Frank Furedi
The Road to Ukraine

De Gruyter
Disruptions

Volume 2

Frank Furedi

The Road to Ukraine

How the West Lost its Way

DE GRUYTER

ISBN (Paperback) 978-3-11-099694-4
ISBN (Hardcover) 978-3-11-099562-6
e-ISBN (PDF) 978-3-11-098154-4
e-ISBN (EPUB) 978-3-11-098175-9
ISSN 2748-9086

Library of Congress Control Number: 2022940543

Bibliographic information published by the Deutsche Nationalbibliothek
The Deutsche Nationalbibliothek lists this publication in the Deutsche Nationalbibliografie;
detailed bibliographic data are available on the Internet at http://dnb.dnb.de.

© 2022 Walter de Gruyter GmbH, Berlin/Boston
Cover image: Fabio Ballasina / unsplash.com
Printing and binding: CPI books GmbH, Leck

www.degruyter.com

Acknowledgements

On the 14 March 2022 I gave a public presentation at a meeting organised by the Academy of Ideas in London on the war in Ukraine and the broader issues surrounding it. The discussion led to a lively debate, one that stimulated me to look into matters further. Had it not been for the comments and criticism made by people at this meeting, I would have never written this book. I am grateful to them for forcing me to develop my thoughts. Tight deadlines are difficult to meet. It was only because of close collaboration with my wife Ann Furedi, son, Jacob Furedi and friends Norman Lewis and D.J. Nolan that the text could see the light of day. They criticised and commented on the text and edited and sub-edited it. I owe a debt of gratitude to their generous intellectual and editing contribution.

Menaggio, Lombardy,
1 June 2022

https://doi.org/10.1515/9783110981544-001

Preface

It is 29 March, 2022, and it has been five weeks since Russia invaded Ukraine. I am standing in front of an old, imposing building in the middle of a small historic city, one that my Hungarian parents referred to as Munkács. Now it is part Ukraine and goes by the title of Mukachevo. The city is in the Zakarpattia Oblast, in Western Ukraine. The traces of the past cultures and ethnic communities that inhabited this place are everywhere: a typed notice in front of a Roman Catholic Church provides information regarding the hours and days of the week when mass is given in Ukrainian, Hungarian and Slovakian.

Most people I talk to are far more interested in complaining about the traffic and the large number of cars that have entered their city since the outbreak of the war than about Russia's invasion of their country. It appears that thousands of Ukrainians from Kyiv and parts of Western Ukraine have decided to drive to the city and stay put until the outcome of this conflict is decided. 'As long as there is hope, we are going to stay in Ukraine,' one lawyer from Kyiv tells me. 'We don't want to become refugees.' A local woman describes the air raid sirens that pierce through the night and how many of her friends with children have decided to make their way to the Hungarian border. With a voice of quiet defiance, she tells me that despite the air raid sirens, 'I am staying – this is my home!'

Munkács/Mukachevo has always been on the frontlines of change in the region. In the early part of the 20th century, it was part of the Austro-Hungarian Empire, but after the First World War, the allies decided to hand the region over to Czechoslovakia. In November 1938, in the wake of the partitioning of Czechoslovakia, it was awarded to Hungary. In 1944, the Soviet Red Army occupied the region. For a brief period, the Soviet Union handed it back to Czechoslovakia before taking direct possession of it in 1945. The same year, the Kremlin ceded Munkács/Mukachevo to the Ukraine Soviet Socialist Republic, which is now known as Ukraine.

During the interwar years Munkács/Mukachevo was often referred to as Little Jerusalem. Almost fifty per cent of its population was Jewish and it became the centre of Judaic culture in the Trans-Carpathian region of what was then Czechoslovakia. By this time there were 30 synagogues serving the heterogeneous Jewish community. But this community was destroyed during the Holocaust and there are only a handful of Jews left in the city[1]. A memorial to the victims

---

1 See https://blogs.timesofisrael.com/ukraine-on-my-mind-though-i-am-not-ukrainian.

https://doi.org/10.1515/9783110981544-002

of the Holocaust at the site of the city's long-gone central synagogue is one of the few reminders of this tragic past.

One reason why I travelled to Ukraine was to find out how a region that has seen so many occupying powers come and go was responding to the latest threat, this time posed by the invading army of Russia. Posters on billboards depicting heroic Ukrainian soldiers indicate that this region is still part of a long tragic drama, whose origins go back to at least the 20th century. At a community centre, where volunteer relief workers are handing out second-hand clothes and food to the long queue of weary refugees, a middle-aged woman, speaking good English, asks me if they can really count on the West. Since I am not sure what to say, I hesitate and before I can formulate my answer, she gives an 'I knew it' look.

In the drama of Munkács my own family figures as bit players. I never had a chance to meet or talk to my grandfather, Ferenc Taub, or to my mother's brother, Imre. During the First World War, my grandfather served in the Hungarian army and fought on the Italian front. He was delighted when illness forced his early return to civilian life in early 1916. He believed that this war was an entirely pointless one, one that did not serve his nation's interest.

Unfortunately, the war did not end for him or my family in 1916. He was taken away in 1944 and forced into a slave labour battalion. When he, along with my Uncle Imre, froze to death somewhere not far from the city, the Second World War was about to reach the final phase of armed conflict. Were he alive today, I suspect he would not be surprised to discover that a durable regime of peace continues to elude the region.

In *The First World War: Still No End In Sight*, I suggested that many of the difficult existential questions that emerged before and during this conflict still remain unresolved[2]. Unlike many commentators who claimed that, with the end of the Cold War, the long war that began in 1914 has finally concluded, I maintained that its legacy continues to influence the contemporary world and find new expressions. The predicament facing Ukraine indicates that the conflicts unleashed during the Great War have not yet exhausted themselves.

It was during the First World War that Ukrainian nationalism became a mass movement. Until then, any aspiration for the establishment of an independent nation was thwarted by the division of the territory that would eventually become Ukraine between the Russian Empire to the east and the Austro-Hungarian Empire to the west. The collapse of these empires during the Great War provided the leaders of the Ukrainian nationalists with an opportunity to seize the moment and establish an independent nation-state.

---

2 Furedi, F. (2014) *The First World War: Still No End In Sight*, Bloomsbury Press: London.

Yet despite gaining momentum and expanding its influence among the people of the region, Ukrainian nationalists failed to realise their objective. Instead, the collapse of the empires was followed by the occupation of the territory of today's Ukraine by the Soviet Union and Poland. Throughout the interwar era most of present-day Ukraine came to be ruled by these two nations. At various times western Ukraine was ruled by Poland, Romania and Czechoslovakia.

In a formal sense Ukraine acquired a geographical existence in 1918 in the territory ruled by the Soviet Union. As one study of Ukraine's history explains, 'under Soviet rule, Ukraine possessed all of the nominal trappings of sovereign statehood, most notably, a full set of republican institutions, like all other Soviet republics'. However, 'in reality the Ukrainian Soviet Socialist Republic was only a hollow institutional caricature of a sovereign state'[3]. With the collapse of the Soviet Union in 1991, Ukraine finally had an opportunity to break free from the Kremlin and declare its independence. However, as subsequent events indicated, it was easier to break free from a disintegrating Soviet Empire than it was to break from the legacy of the past. Russia invaded Ukraine in 2014 and succeeded in annexing Crimea and occupied a large chunk of territory on the other side of its border with eastern Ukraine.

The geographical divisions imposed on the territory of Ukraine by competing powers and the cultural tensions between Russian and Ukrainian-speaking citizens made it difficult to establish a coherent sense of national identity. What one historian calls 'competing "grand narratives of the past"' have retained a degree of salience.[4] In such circumstances Moscow could project itself as the defender of the Russian-speaking minority in Ukraine. In this way, Russia attempted to ensure that it retained a degree of influence over the conduct of Ukraine's domestic affairs.

Russia's decision to invade Ukraine in February 2022 was motivated by a variety of different factors which remain a subject of lively controversy. At the time of writing, it is still far from clear how this war will end. But, looking at the map today – with Russian forces occupying parts of eastern and southern Ukraine – it bears an uncanny resemblance to how it looked in 1914 when this territory was partitioned by two declining empires. It feels as if the current situation is a continuation of the one that burst on the scene in 1914.

The aim of this book is to remind readers that, contrary to the prejudice that history has ended, we remain under the spell of the past. This is a lesson that

---

3 See Wolczuk, K. (2001) *The moulding of Ukraine: the constitutional politics of state formation*, Central European University Press: Budapest. https://books.openedition.org/ceup/1739?lang=en.
4 von Hagen, M. (1995) 'Does Ukraine Have a History?', *Slavic Review*, vol. 54, p. 667.

western cultural and political influencers have chosen to disregard, which is why they were so unable to understand the chain of events that led to the invasion of Ukraine.

The war that broke out in February 2022 is no longer just about the future of Ukraine. It erupted at a time of great global upheaval following the trauma caused by the outbreak of a deadly pandemic. It also coincided with the emergence of an economic nationalism that threatened to exacerbate problems caused by shortages of natural resources and the unravelling of supply chains. Ukraine has become an involuntary conduit through which these global issues are experienced – a warning that neither our peace nor our security can be taken for granted.

One of the aims of this book is to explain that the problems that confront us are not only the invading armies of Russia but also the historical illiteracy and moral confusion of the West. The danger is that, unwittingly, Western leaders' response to this invasion could lead the crisis in Ukraine into a slow *danse macabre* that envelops the whole world. The subtitle of this book is *How The West Lost Its Way*, a reference to the loss of direction that is intimately linked to the failure of Western society to take seriously its historical legacy. The relative absence of a consciousness of history deprived the West of the guidance necessary for engaging with new experiences. The war in Ukraine provides an important opportunity for the West to finally learn that it has to come to terms with the past.

Some of my friends and colleagues have warned me that I am taking a big risk by writing this book while the war is going on and before we know of its final outcome. My reply to them – to paraphrase Graham Greene – is that this is a 'story which has no beginning or end'.

Contents

Chapter 1
The Revenge of History

One of the momentous consequences of Russia's invasion of Ukraine is that it has forced thinking people to look history straight in the face. How else can we make sense of this unexpected and apparently senseless conflict? Wars are supposed to happen in Africa and the Middle East, but not in Europe. In recent decades promoters of the ideology of globalism tended to assume that Europe has turned into a war-free zone. As one commentary titled 'Why has war become obsolete in Europe?' noted in the pre-war era of 2010, 'it is quite remarkable that a continent, which for much of its modern history was embroiled in internecine warfare, now seems to be one of the most stable regions of the world[5].

In recent decades, much has been written about how global economic integration would make wars between nations less likely. Other commentators reflected on how European integration offered a permanent 'solution to war'[6]. Some scholars went so far as to claim that war has become obsolescent[7]. In his *The Remnants Of War*, John Mueller contends that developed nations have gone beyond war, and militarised conflict has tended to be reduced to 'thugs' who are residual combatants.

This form of magical thinking about wars has led some international relations experts to distinguish between old and new conflicts. The kind of war raging in Ukraine is characterised as an 'old war' by Mary Kaldor. She describes old wars as a 'stereotyped version of war drawn from the experience of the last centuries in Europe'. These wars – which are not supposed to happen – are the ones between two sovereign states[8]. New wars are portrayed as hybrid conflicts between for example, state and non-state networks.

The idea that old wars are an anachronism has even captured the imagination of some policymakers in charge of their nation's security. Back in 2014, the American Secretary of State John Kerry reacted to Russia's first invasion of Ukraine by stating that Moscow was behaving like it was the 19th century. 'You just don't in the 21st century behave in 19th-century fashion by invading another

---

5 https://spice.fsi.stanford.edu/docs/why_war_has_become_obsolete_in_europe
6 Eilstrup-Sangiovanni, M. and Verdier, D. (2005) 'European integration as a solution to war', *European Journal of International Relations*, vol. 11.
7 Mueller, J. (2004) The remnants of war, Cornell University Press: Ithaca.
8 https://www.stabilityjournal.org/articles/10.5334/sta.at/
   This argument is developed in Kaldor, M. (1999) *New and Old Wars: Organised Violence in a Global Era*, Polity Press: Cambridge.

https://doi.org/10.1515/9783110981544-003

country on completely trumped up pre-text,' Kerry said[9]. Such a naïve association of armed aggression with the 19th century revealed not only a profound misunderstanding of the past, but also an alarming ignorance of *realpolitik*. As an
editorial in the *Wall Street Journal*, ironically titled, 'Welcome to the 19th Century',
responded to Kerry: 'Though he didn't intend it, the U.S. Secretary of State was
summing up the difference between the current leaders of the West who inhabit
a fantasy world of international rules and the hard men of the Kremlin who understand the language of power'[10].

It is likely that now, after Russia launched its second invasion of Russia, the
Kerrys of this world have finally become dispossessed of their illusions. Suddenly all the utopian and impressionistic accounts acclaiming the obsolescence of
wars have given way to concerns about the return of old-fashioned military conflicts between nation-states. 'War in Europe is no longer unthinkable' conclude
two international relations experts, Ivan Krastev and Mark Leonard[11]. This sentiment is echoed by authors of 'An Appeal for Civic Action in Europe and Beyond',
who assert that 'another war in Europe no longer seems improbable or unlikely'[12].

Magical thinking about the obsolescence of wars in Europe was promoted by
advocates of the ideology of globalisation. Obituaries to the phenomenon of war
between European nations were also regularly issued by ideologues promoting
the federalist project of the European Union. In 2012, the EU was awarded the
Nobel Peace Prize. Four years later, the claim that the EU is the only guarantor
of peace in Europe was a key argument promoted by the Remainer lobby in the
debate around Brexit in the United Kingdom[13]. They insisted that, in the EU, the
rule of law replaced the crude projection of the power of the nation-state.

The war in Ukraine should serve as a wake-up call. Nevertheless, numerous
commentators still insist on associating wars with a bygone age. Thus Roger
Cohen, the foreign editor of *The New York Times* commented:

'The confrontation is between 19th- and 21st-century worldviews, with potential consequences that the 20th century illustrated at Verdun, Hiroshima and elsewhere. Mr. Putin's war in

---

9 https://www.politico.com/blogs/politico-now/2014/03/kerry-russia-behaving-like-its-the-19th-
century-184280.
10 https://www.wsj.com/articles/welcome-to-the-19th-century-1395009669?tesla=y.
11 https://ecfr.eu/publication/the-crisis-of-european-security-what-europeans-think-about-the-
war-in-ukraine/
12 https://www.anothereurope.org/no-more-war-in-europe/
13 https://www.london4europe.co.uk/why_we_are_remainers_how_we_will_remain.

Ukraine has demonstrated that the risk of great conflagrations has not been consigned to the past'[14].

Wars are indeed horrible. But to imagine that they are somehow confined to the worldview of the 19th century not only smacks of a form of wilful historical amnesia but also of self-deception. Wars in the 21st century may have been fought outside the Western world but, like in Verdun, the battlefields were left soaked with blood. The more than 350,000 people killed in the wars over the future of Syria are testament to the tragic realities of 21st-century warfare.

The tendency to treat 'old wars' in Europe as a historical anachronism is closely linked to what the international security expert Andrew Michta described as the weakening of the consensus that the 'nation-state should remain paramount in world politics'[15]. The belittling of national sovereignty as an outdated prejudice that has become irrelevant in a globalised world was widely internalised by the Western political and cultural establishment. As Michta noted, the authority of the nation-state has been increasingly brought into question. This view is most explicitly conveyed by academic cosmopolitan theorists, who regard their crusade against nationalism as the historical equivalent of the struggle against religious superstition in the early modern era. 'Just as Christian theology had to be repressed at the start of the Modern Period in Europe, the political sphere of action must be opened up today anew by taming nationalist theology,' advises one of the foremost exponents of cosmopolitanism, the late German sociologist Ulrich Beck[16].

The historical amnesia that afflicts Western cosmopolitan and globalist thought was intertwined with the cultural sensibility of historical closure and terminus. As if the world has become liberated from its past, the cosmopolitan worldview continually perceives reality as novel and new. This is an outlook that has turned its obsession with novelty into an ideology of 'Endism'. In his study *Politics and Fate* (2013) the political theorist Andrew Gamble wrote about the 'outbreak of "endism"'[17]. If one were to believe all the claims made on this score, it would be difficult to avoid the conclusion that just about everything that mattered in the days of the old normal has come to an end. While some writers have reflected on the end of old wars, others have declared the End of History or The End of Ideology or The End of The Nation-State. There

---

14 https://www.nytimes.com/2022/05/07/world/europe/putin-victory-day-macron.html

15 https://www.the-american-interest.com/2017/07/01/losing-nation-state/

16 See interview with Beck in *SightandSound*, 20 November 2007, http://www.signandsight.com/features/1603.html.

17 Gamble, A. (2013) *Politics and Fate*, Wiley: London.

are books considering the end of sovereignty, the end of authority, the end of the West and the end of politics. Commentators declare 'the end of the book', which will hopefully materialise after you have finished this text[18]. Even science is recruited to the cause of endism by the author of *The End of Science: Facing The Limits Of Knowledge In The Twilight Of The Scientific Age*[19]. Numerous commentators reflect on the end of the world and wonder 'how the world ends'[20].

As I note later in this book, an obsession with endism reflects an aspiration to break with the past and be done with history. During the mid-1970s, the American historian Christopher Lasch observed that 'we are fast losing the sense of historical continuity, the sense of belonging to a succession of generations originating in the past and stretching into the future'[21]. Since the 1970s, the loss of the sense of historical continuity has mutated into a consciously incited form of historical amnesia. The historian Tony Judt warned that of 'all our contemporary illusions, the most dangerous is the one that underpins and accounts for all the others. And that is the idea that we live in a time without precedent: that what is happening to us is new and irreversible and that the past has nothing to teach us'[22].

The pervasive sense of historical amnesia was explicitly fostered in the EU through the promotion of a version of year zero history. This sentiment even dominates the teaching of history, where often anything that precedes the end of the Second World War is portrayed as the 'bad old days'. From this standpoint, 1945 is Year Zero and anything that precedes it is interpreted through the prism of scepticism and malevolence. Thus, the EU-funded House of History in Brussels decided to leave behind Europe's historical past by settling on 1946 as the EU's year zero[23]. In all but name year zero suggested that the bad old days of wars, atrocities and destructive ideologies were left behind through the institutionalisation of European integration.

This narrative which emerged in the 1950s told a tale of how the original member states of the EU emerged phoenix-like from the ashes of the war to renounce nationalism as a basis for conducting relations between states. According to this version of events, European unity was responsible for transcending

18 https://www.theatlantic.com/magazine/archive/1994/09/the-end-of-the-book/376361/
19 Horgan, J. (2015) *The End of Science*, Basic Books: New York.
20 https://www.livescience.com/65633-climate-change-dooms-humans-by-2050.html
21 Lasch, C. (2018) *The culture of narcissism: American life in an age of diminishing expectations*, WW Norton & Company: New York, p. 246.
22 Judt, T. (2009) *Reappraisals: Reflections On A Forgotten Century*, Vintage Books: London, p. 19.
23 https://www.civitas.org.uk/2011/04/07/rewriting-history/

the nationalist conflicts that had led to numerous wars – and also for creating the conditions for economic prosperity in the post-Second World War period. From this standpoint, the achievement of European unity was portrayed as a secular equivalent of biblical redemption. In this story, European federalism symbolised a sacred cause while identification with a nation was assigned the role of a form of political heresy.

One of the unfortunate consequences of this myth of redemption that saw Europe rising like a phoenix from the ashes was that it went beyond the renunciation of the dark era of 1914 – 1945, and instead led to the repudiation of much of the past. Europe's pre-1945 past was increasingly depicted in negative terms. In part, this attitude was a reaction to the abuse of history by politically motivated nationalist historians during the previous two centuries. It also expressed the concern that dwelling too closely into the pre-1945 era would exacerbate conflict between member states and other European nations.

The EU's cultural and educational initiatives constantly peddled a simplistic account of history that made little attempt to educate people on the legacy of European civilisation. By settling on 1946 as Europe's Year Zero, the EU political elite sought to free itself from a history that it neither appreciates nor understands. A political culture that appears to be so embarrassed by its past is unlikely to succeed in communicating its cultural legacy to the younger generation. Consequently, any young person embarking on the study of the past could easily gain the conviction that Europe was born in the aftermath of 1945.

For the EU educational establishment, the history of the continent before 1946 is alien, if not hostile, territory. Of course, European history contains its fair share of depressing and horrific episodes. And it is entirely understandable that many enlightened Europeans wish to do everything they can to eliminate the regressive influences of aggressive nationalism and xenophobia. But, like it or not, Europe is stuck with its past and it cannot go forward unless it reckons with it.

Not surprisingly, some historians have gone so far as to claim that the people of Europe have become psychically distanced from the past to such an extent that they no longer need history to cultivate their identity or to make sense of who they are. 'Clearly Europeans have a sense of themselves as survivors of a history they have left far behind them; they do not see history as their origin or the foundation on which they stand', argued the German historian Christian Meier. He added:

> 'History is not something they desire to carry on (in a better way if possible), Hence they feel no gratitude to their forebears for what they achieved with so much labour; on the contrary, they are fixated on all the things they don't understand (and are making an effort to

understand), such as wars, injustice, discrimination against women, slavery, and the like. They feel uncoupled from their history, the seriousness of which they are, generally speaking, less and less able to imagine'[24].

As evidence of this trend, Meier cites the attempt of the EU to distance itself from Europe's historical past. 'Thus, as far as I can see, the European Union is emerging as the first political entity of the modern era that has no need for its own history and for a historical orientation', states Meier[25]. Experience indicates that the EU's indifference to history has deprived it of an ability to understand the present. Judt's reflection on the propensity 'to deny the relevance of past experience to present problems' is particularly salient for understanding why so many experts and commentators were caught unaware by the momentum leading to Russia's invasion of Ukraine[26].

A disregard of historical continuity that characterised the outlook of Western cultural elites has had far less of a purchase in the former satellite states of the Soviet Union. Decades of totalitarian oppression still remain fresh in people's minds. It is not just in Ukraine that people are acutely sensitive to the precarious status of their national independence. For Ukrainians, there is little that is senseless about the current war. Many remember previous attempts by Russia to wrest control of their nation. They remember the pact signed at Yalta by the leaders of the Soviet Union, Britain and the United States in 1945 – an agreement that led to the division of Europe between its Western and Eastern blocs. They remember that this pact assigned them the role of an abject colony of Moscow.

Just over three decades ago another apparently senseless conflict erupted in Europe, this time in the Balkans. When asked about his reaction to the outburst of ethnic warfare in his country, the veteran Yugoslav dissident Milovan Djilas remarked that 'communism was just a temporary episode in our history'[27]. What Djilas meant was that not even a ruthless communist dictatorship could undo and break the thread linking the Balkan's past with its present. History took its revenge through the dramatic break-up of Yugoslavia. Were he alive today, it is likely that he would reiterate his point in response to the catastrophe inflicted by Russia on Ukraine. Unlike the advocates of the influential versions of

---

24 Meier, C. (2005) *The Uses of History: From Athens to Auschwitz*, Harvard University Press: Cambridge, Mass., p. 17.
25 Meier (2005), p. 17.
26 Judt (2009), p. 22.
27 Cited in *The Guardian*, 13 July 1991, http://arhiv.mm.gov.si/vlada/20/tuji/1991_13_07_The_Guardian_Division_of_Bosnia_could_hold_key.pdf

the dogma of year zero history, Djilas understood that the present cannot be entirely sealed off from the past.

Djilas' warning about the enduring salience of the past is tragically vindicated by the terrible events unfolding in Ukraine. It certainly feels like history has woken up and decided to impose its will on the people of Russia, Ukraine and nearby nations. It has upended the prevailing global order and called into question the post-Cold War balance of power in Europe. Vladimir Putin has weaponised history to legitimate his expansionist ambitions. In order to inspire and mobilise the people of Russia, Putin constantly appeals to the lessons of history. His speeches communicate his imperial ambition through a wide-ranging discourse on Russia's past[28]. Some of his speeches dwell on events that supposedly occurred over a thousand years ago.

It is simply not possible to understand Russia's invasion and the Ukrainian response to it without understanding the historical dynamic that led to this conflict. As the author of 'The Politics of History in and Around Ukraine, 1980s-2010s', Georgiy Kasianov observed in *Foreign Affairs*, 'Europe's first twenty-first-century war is very much about the past[29]. Kasianov notes that:

> 'Russian forces have been smashing their way through Ukraine for over two months now, spurred in large part by historical fiction. But history also propels the fierce Ukrainian resistance. Ukrainians, too, harbor a particular understanding of the past that motivates them to fight. In many ways, this war is the collision of two incompatible historical narratives.'

The politicisation of memory by both sides of this conflict highlights the enduring influence of history in motivating the behaviour of the main protagonists in the war. That is why the war can be described – at least in part – as 'the collision of pasts'.

In Putin's version of events, Ukraine is historically indistinguishable from Russia. On Kyiv, Putin cites Oleg the Prophet saying in the 10th century, 'Let it be the mother of all Russian cities'. A view often expressed by Western commentators is that Putin is merely using history rather than really believing his rhetoric[30]. What matters, however, is not whether or not Putin is 'using history', but the fact that he has decided to inspire his supporters through drawing on the resources provided by his version of Russia's past.

---

28 See for example http://en.kremlin.ru/events/president/news/66181
29 Kasianov, G. 'The War Over Ukrainian Identity', *Foreign Affairs*, 4 May 2022, https://www.foreignaffairs.com/articles/ukraine/2022-05-04/war-over-ukrainian-identity#author-info
30 See for example the discussion in https://www.theatlantic.com/international/archive/2022/02/putin-russia-ukraine-revisionist-history/622936/

A Very Different Sense of the Past

Putin's veneration of Russia's Golden Past stands in sharp contrast to the indifference of Western political leaders towards their national past. That's one reason why they don't understand or at least refuse to comprehend the way that Putin's sense of historical mission influences his geo-political calculations. Unlike Putin, his Western counterparts are embarrassed about the history of their nation. Especially in the Anglo-American world, an anti-historical consensus prevails among its political and cultural establishment.

It is very difficult to entirely ignore the past. Nevertheless, since the 1980s there has been a discernible trend towards the attempt to decouple the present from the past. In part this trend is fuelled by the palpable sense of estrangement Western society has from its historical legacy. Such sentiments are not confined to the radical postmodernist. Even mainstream liberal and conservative thought in the West has become emotionally disconnected from the past. Thus, in reference to racist incidents in football, the former British Conservative Prime Minister David Cameron could declare in February 2012 that 'we will not let recent events drag us back to the bad old days of the past'[31]. His use of the phrase 'bad old days' constituted more than a response to a single ugly incident. It suggested that as far as he was concerned there was little worthwhile to 'conserve' from Britain's past.

As is the case with Russia, in the Western world the past has become the target of ideological plunder. But whereas in Russia the past is worshipped and idealised in the Anglo-American world it is condemned and its history has acquired an accusatory tone. Many of its historic monuments and symbols are vandalised, defaced or destroyed altogether. In the Anglo-American world, the national flag is frequently treated with derision and denounced by leading members of its cultural institutions as symbols of racism, oppression and discrimination. In the UK flag waving had gone out of fashion and the main institutions of British culture have tended to exhibit a sense of defensive embarrassment about any display of patriotism.

Unease towards the legacy of the past is most pronounced within leftist and liberal opinion. That scepticism towards the relevance of the legacy of the past unites virtually all sections of the Western intelligentsia was strikingly affirmed by Gareth Stedman Jones, a former member of the editorial board of the *New Left Review*, when he wrote:

---

31 https://www.theguardian.com/football/2012/feb/22/david-cameron-government-racism-football

'The once magical invocation of history's numinous and redemptive powers now looks either tawdry or sinister. From Passchendaele to Auschwitz, from the Gulag to Hiroshima, and so on to the Killing Fields, the twentieth century has remorselessly torn away from us all remaining vestiges of a simple nineteenth century faith in progress'[32].

Not all accounts of the past are as negative as that of Stedman Jones but within Western culture – popular and positive accounts of a nation's history are conspicuously rare. The usage of the term 'Victorian Values' or 'Victorian morality' in Britain often conveys the connotation of narrow-minded and bigoted attitudes, a rigid social code of conduct, an unhealthy culture of sexual restraint and the scandal of child labour.

There is more than a hint of triumphalism amongst opponents of Britishness when they declare that this nation faces a crisis of identity. 'There's no cohesive British identity anymore, if there ever was' declares a columnist in *The Irish Times*[33]. One fervent opponent of Britishness, the *Guardian* columnist Afua Hirsch, has written an entire book devoted to delegitimising Britain's identity. What all these critics of the attempt to celebrate British identity hold in common is the view that people should avoid taking pride in their culture and their past because there is little to be proud of.

A negative and even hostile representation of Britain and its past is widely promoted by its own media, institutions of education and popular culture. Such sentiments continually call into question the legitimacy of Britain itself. In particular, Britain's history is depicted as a source of embarrassment and of shame. Whereas in the past, schoolchildren were taught about the 'good old days' today they only learn about the 'bad old days' of their society. Consequently, their education encourages them to become estranged from their community and from its cultural legacy.

The cultural crusade against Britishness is rarely challenged. Occasionally, the sense of frustration at the derision directed against a particular British custom leads to a backlash. Recently, the outcry provoked by the BBC's announcement that Rule Britannia will not be sung at the Proms is an example of such a reaction. However, experience shows that a backlash is rarely able to match the force to which it reacts. It is entirely reactive and defensive.

The campaign to undermine the moral status of Britain has been so remarkably successful because the field of battle on which this cultural conflict is fought out has been abandoned by the elites that once defended it. A significant

---

32 Cited in *The Independent*, 28 April 1990.
33 https://www.irishtimes.com/life-and-style/people/jennifer-o-connell-there-s-no-cohesive-british-identity-anymore-if-there-ever-was-1.3835130

section of the British establishment feels detached from its own culture and past. The principal cultural institutions that create and communicate ideas – the universities, the media, the church – have lost the capacity to generate loyalty and pride towards the society that they are meant to serve. In many instances they feel alienated from the historical legacy of Britain to the point that they often unwittingly, but sometimes consciously, communicate the proposition that the attempt to defend Britain is itself indefensible.

The attitude of contempt towards the legacy of the past has played an important role in undermining the capacity of the Western foreign policy establishment to understand the outlook of a society like Russia's, which still takes its history seriously. Back in 2014, Henry Kissinger, former National Security Advisor and Secretary of State under Presidents Nixon and Ford, warned policymakers about the danger of failing to grasp the influence of the past on Russia's outlook on the situation in Ukraine. Writing in the *Washington Post*, Kissinger warned Russia against attempting to 'force Ukraine into a satellite status'[34]. At the same time, he alerted his Western readers to take seriously the lessons of history. He wrote that:

'the West must understand that, to Russia, Ukraine can never be just a foreign country. Russian history began in what was called Kievan-Rus. The Russian religion spread from there. Ukraine has been part of Russia for centuries, and their histories were intertwined before then. Some of the most important battles for Russian freedom, starting with the Battle of Poltava in 1709, were fought on Ukrainian soil. The Black Sea Fleet – Russia's means of projecting power in the Mediterranean – is based by long-term lease in Sevastopol, in Crimea. Even such famed dissidents as Aleksandr Solzhenitsyn and Joseph Brodsky insisted that Ukraine was an integral part of Russian history and, indeed, of Russia[35].

Unlike the present-day cohort of foreign policy experts who inhabit the American State Department or the British Foreign Office, Kissinger possessed a profound understanding of the relationship between geopolitics and the salience of the past. Kissinger observed that 'Putin is a serious strategist – on the premises of Russian history'. Putin's essay 'On The Historical Unity of Russians and Ukrainians' published in July 2021 indicated the powerful pull that history exercises on his imagination. However, as Kissinger indicated, 'understanding U.S. values and psychology are not his strong suits'. At the same time, he concluded that 'understanding Russian history and psychology' has not 'been a strong point of U.S. policymakers'[36].

---

34 Kissinger, H.A. 'How the Ukraine Crisis Ends', *The Washington Post*, 6 March 2014.
35 Kissinger, H.A. 'How the Ukraine Crisis Ends', *The Washington Post*, 6 March 2014.
36 Kissinger, H.A. 'How the Ukraine Crisis Ends', *The Washington Post*, 6 March 2014.

It is worth reflecting on Kissinger's assessment of Russian-Ukrainian relations. Although written eight years ago, it anticipated the potential for a tragedy of historical proportions if the different sides failed to grasp the forces of history that could fuel a conflict. The lack of Western sensitivity to Russia's security concerns is not an inconsiderable factor in the chain of events that led to the invasion of Ukraine. Putin and the Russian government bear direct responsibility for the tragedy inflicted on Ukraine. But a deeper sense of history by the West might have helped restrain Russia. It might have helped if NATO countries were more in touch with Russia's strategic sensitivity to potential threats on its western borders. Germany's invasion of Russia through its western borders during World War Two still haunts this nation's historical memory. A more sophisticated grasp of this memory on Russia's behaviour would at the very least helped prepare the West for dealing with the consequences of the war.

The Long Road to Ukraine

The tragic events in Ukraine remind us history cannot be unmade and that, sooner or later, we have to come to terms with its inescapable truth. Back in 2014, when I published *First World War: Still No End In Sight*, many commentators sniggered at the suggestion that the legacy of this bloody conflict could continue to exercise any influence over our lives[37]. Several pointed to the end of the Cold War as an expression of what they characterised as the end of history. Obituaries to a forever lost conflict-ridden past were frequently communicated through declaring that this is the End. The historian Mark Mazower stated that with the collapse of the Soviet Union in 1989, 'not only the Cold War but the whole era of ideological rivalries which began in 1917 came to an end'[38]. Yet, what he described as 'the unremitting struggle' to 'define modern Europe' continues to be reflected in bitter conflicts over values and culture-and in the blood shed over the future of Ukraine.

Almost unannounced, the kind of war that many Europeans believed would no longer blight their continent has suddenly erupted with a vengeance. Some interpret this war as heralding the end of the 'Old World Order'[39]. This interpretation reflects an illusion about the stability of the globalist post-Cold War era. The war in Ukraine indicates that despite the Western commentariat's best ef-

---

37 Furedi, F. (2014) *First World War: Still No End In Sight*, Bloomsbury: London.
38 Mazower, M. (1999) *Dark Continent: Europe's Twentieth Century*, Penguin Book: London, p. X.
39 See https://www.theatlantic.com/international/archive/2022/02/us-europe-russia-putin-new-world/622917/

forts, we are not done with the past. The very difficult questions raised and re-raised during a succession of violent conflicts are still in search of satisfactory answers.

No End in Sight

Events in Ukraine and the confusions about geopolitical matters sweeping the Western world are not unconnected to the forces of history unleashed during the early decades of the 20th century. The chain of events that followed in the wake of the First World War continues to disrupt life in the 21st century. It is important to underline that the great wars of the 20th century were not simply motivated by geopolitical concerns. Domestic issues and ideological commitments intertwined with national interests and were affirmed on the field of battle. Domestic politics mixed seamlessly with interstate relations.[40]. Moreover, conflicts over values were embedded in the consciousness of many people who were motivated to fight a war. Idealism motivated millions. Subsequent disappointment regarding the failure to realise these ideals intensified a tendency towards the kind of moral disorientation that pervades society today.

The decisive geopolitical conflicts of the 20th century had a significant influence on the moral, intellectual and political outlook of the Western world. There were three decisive episodes that have had a powerful impact on domestic politics and on the conduct of public life. One important outcome of the Second World War was that it led to the erosion of the moral authority of the Right. The political Right was forced on the defensive as its intellectual and political credibility was seriously undermined. In turn, the Cold War fundamentally discredited most of the ideals and practices associated with the Left. Since the 1980s, those who perceive themselves as Right and Left often struggle to give meaning to their political outlook. Neither side has succeeded in recovering the idealism and intellectual conviction that motivated their political ancestors.

The impact of the Second World War and of the Cold War on ideologies and political identities has been widely discussed by proponents of the 'end-of-ideology' thesis. What these commentaries overlook or underestimate is the legacy of the third episode, which is the more than century-long Culture War. To put the argument in its baldest form: the main target of the Culture War was the legacy of the past. It always sought to distance society from its past and by implication

40 Mayer, A.J. (1969) 'Internal Causes and Purposes of War in Europe, 1870–1956: A Research Assignment', *The Journal of Modern History*, vol. 41, no. 3, pp. 291–303.

attempted to diminish the capacity of Western culture to think historically. Claims about the 'end of history' are underpinned by the sensibility that history has ended or been left behind. It was precisely the belief that history could be suppressed or bypassed that led so many leading experts and commentators to draw the conclusion that Europe and the West was now more or less a war-free zone. From this perspective, bloody conflicts were confined to places like Syria or Afghanistan. Apparently, the end of history exempted the West from ever having to confront such conflicts within its own borders.

After the invasion of Ukraine, there can be no doubt that history cannot be left behind. A recent front cover of *Time* magazine depicts a Russian tank rolling into Ukraine and has as its headline 'The Return of History'[41]. In reality, history never went away, and the fantasy of a post-history world has been cruelly exposed by events in Ukraine.

Some write of the ghost of the past or the 'ghosts' of Europe's 'terrible 20th century returning to Ukraine' but, as I explain in the chapters that follow, the past is not a ghost. It is very real. The past could not be killed off by repeating the phrase that 'we are at the end of history'[42].

Traces of the long road that leads to the battlefields of Ukraine could already be detected during the years leading up to the arrival of the 20th century. No one captured the cultural zeitgeist that prevailed in the years leading to the outbreak of the first World War better than the novelist Joseph Roth. Born in 1894, in Brody, a small Galician town in what today is Lviv Oblast in western Ukraine, Roth embarked on a literary pilgrimage across a seemingly barren landscape of a conflict-ridden European history. Joseph Roth's novel *Radetzky March* takes us on a journey that begins in the secure world of Emperor Franz Joseph and moves on to the terrain that will soon see the collapse of the Austro-Hungarian Empire. The book conveys an atmosphere where an irresistible force ruptures people's links with the security of their taken-for-granted assumptions. The main characters are swept up by events that will lead Europe to embark on a suicidal conflict – the First World War. But that is not the end of our story.

Just like the chaos and displacement that runs through the *Radetzky March*, the sense of security in an independent Ukrainian nation has been shattered by forces beyond its citizens' control. Their experience reminds us that the issues thrown up in the past remain unresolved.

---

41 https://twitter.com/TIME/status/1497010566581346307

42 https://www.irishtimes.com/opinion/editorial/the-irish-times-view-on-the-invasion-of-ukraine-ghosts-from-a-terrible-past-1.4812264

Over a century later, when I talk to Ukrainian refugees passing through Hungary in search of of a secure haven, I cannot help but feel that I am in the middle of the latest edition of *Radetzky March*. A mixture of anxiety, despair and hope was painted on their faces as they queued up in front of the Help Tent, opposite the Budapest Western railway station. Two teenage boys approached me when they saw me taking notes. "Tell them that it is not just about our freedom but that it is also personal," one said.

It was also very personal for me: not just because I was bearing witness to an unfolding human tragedy but because of the realisation that I had been here before. I was nine when the Soviet army crushed the 1956 Hungarian Revolution. My family was forced to flee our home and cross the border to Austria. Rather naively in the decades to follow, we came to believe that finally we have entered an era of peace. Now it feels like the bad old days have returned to haunt Ukraine and the surrounding region. Yet again, a palpable mood of insecurity prevails.

When I chat to elderly Hungarians about Russia's invasion of Ukraine, I often get treated to a history lesson. In a tone of resignation, Márton, an 86-year old pensioner who grew up in a Magyar community on the Ukrainian side of the border, reminds me that ever since the Russian army helped crush the Hungarian Revolutionary War in 1848, 'we have always lived under the shadow of war'. He adds: 'the Russians came for us in 1956... Who knows when all this will stop?' His friend Csaba interrupts with a chilling reminder, 'history never goes to sleep'.

Yet unlike Csaba and Márton, for whom history is very real, the Western cultural and power elites who have the potential power to influence the course of global developments continue to suffer from the condition of historical amnesia. They are not quite sure how they got to a world where the invasion of a sovereign European nation has become a fact of life. Without the guidance of the past, they appear lost and bereft of strategic insight. An as ever, the danger is that those suffering from the condition of historical amnesia may inadvertently sleepwalk into more dangerous territory.

Chapter 2
In Search of Legitimacy

That the West lost its way on the long historical road leading to the battlefields of Ukraine was strikingly illustrated by a *mea culpa* issued by Robert Reich, President Bill Clinton's former Secretary of Labor. Reich admitted that 'he was wrong about the 21st century'[43]. He used to think that nationalism was disappearing, democracy is inevitable, and a nuclear war could not happen. 'I expected globalization would blur borders, create economic interdependence among nations and regions and extend a modern consumer and artistic culture worldwide', he wrote. Like many members of the Western cultural establishment, Reich assumed that in a globalised world 'advanced nations will no longer go to war over geographical territory'.

Reich's naïve grasp of geopolitical realities is widely shared by the political and cultural elites who influence and direct foreign policy in Washington, London, Paris and Berlin, as well as in the less powerful Western nations. This naivety is a symptom of what I take to be the principal cultural disease of our time- which is that of historical amnesia. Like Reich, numerous experts and policy-makers regard Russia's invasion as an alarm call that forces them to catch up with the realities of a new era. However, it often seems that they are not so much catching up with present-day realities but rather very slowly catching up with the past.

Historical amnesia desensitises people from an awareness of how things change over time. It deprives them of an essential understanding of historical specificity and produces confusion regarding the relation between historical continuity and change. Historical amnesia frequently runs in parallel with a triumphalist sensibility regarding the supposed superiority of the 'now'; i.e. current attitudes and practices. It regards the past as a stage that is morally inferior to the present. From this standpoint the 'bad old days' are best left behind. Traces of this ahistorical sensibility were evident throughout the 20th century. However, they acquired an unmistakably triumphalist tone during the final phase of the Cold War. Some Western commentators went so far as to declare that history has ended and that the collapse of the Soviet Union represented the beginning of a peaceful New World Order. On several occasions, President

43 https://www.theguardian.com/commentisfree/2022/mar/13/putin-trump-ukraine-russia-invasion-war-21st-century

https://doi.org/10.1515/9783110981544-004

George H. W. Bush spoke about the emergence of a New World Order[44]. In an address to a joint session of Congress on 11 September, 1990, he delivered a speech titled 'Toward a New World Order', stating:

> 'Now, we can see a new world coming into view. A world in which there is the genuine prospect of new world order'[45].

He sounded positively euphoric on this score in his State of the Union address in 1992. 'The biggest thing that has happened in the world in my life, in our lives, is this: by the grace of God, America won the Cold War', he told the joint session of Congress[46]. Referring to 'changes of almost biblical proportions', Bush boasted that 'a world once divided into two armed camps now recognizes one sole and preeminent power, the United States of America'.

Others too embraced the globalist vision of a New World Order that marked a radical break from the bad old days of the past. 'Mine is the first generation able to contemplate the possibility that we may live our entire lives without going to war or sending our children to war, claimed former British Prime Minister, Tony Blair in 1997, in a speech at a NATO-Russia summit in Paris[47] . Like Robert Reich, Blair assumed that wars – at least in Europe – were an anachronism. 'A new European landscape is being reclaimed from the battlegrounds of the 20th century' argued Blair. As the international relations scholar Christopher Coker reminds us, Blair 'spoke with the confidence of a man who knew little history.' Blair 'went on to fight five wars'. He 'soon found out that we do not live only in the present: during our lives the past is constantly relived or renegotiated. He failed to grasp the power of the past to contaminate the present'[48].

The failure to understand and come to terms with the power of the past to influence the present continues to haunt the corridors of power of Western governments. In echoing Bush's claim of the rise of an American-led New World Order, President Joe Biden indicated that he has learned nothing and forgotten nothing. In a speech delivered to business leaders in March 2022, Biden declared; 'now is a time when things are shifting. There's going to be a new world order and we have got to lead it and we have got to unite the rest of

---

44 https://www.washingtonpost.com/archive/politics/1990/09/12/bush-out-of-these-troubled-times-a-new-world-order/b93b5cf1-e389-4e6a-84b0-85f71bf4c946.

45 https://bush41library.tamu.edu/archives/public-papers/2217

46 https://www.nytimes.com/1992/01/29/us/state-union-transcript-president-bush-s-address-state-union.html

47 https://www.ukpol.co.uk/tony-blair-1997-speech-in-paris.

48 Coker, C. (2009) *War In An Age of Risk*, Polity Press: Cambridge, p. vii.

the free world in doing it'[49]. Having presided over America's humiliating withdrawal from Afghanistan, Biden seized upon the tragic events in Ukraine as an opportunity to remind the world of his nation's faded global hegemony.

Biden's historical amnesia is compounded by a stupefying ignorance of geopolitical realities. The kind of geopolitical illiteracy that led Biden to confuse Ukrainians with Iranians speaks to a political culture that regards wars fought abroad as an opportunity to acclaim a new version of a Washington-led New World Order[50]. No wonder that policymakers in Washington are dreaming of reinventing a new version of the Cold War strategy of containment[51]. It appears that they believe that mobilising the Western world to isolate Russia would strengthen America's claim for global leadership. That is why Washington sought to transform what began as a war between Russia and Ukraine into a conflict that pits Washington more directly against Moscow. Towards the end of April 2022, the American Defense Secretary, Lloyd J. Austin, declared that Washington's goal was to see Russia so 'weakened' that it would no longer have the power to invade a neighbouring state[52]. In all but name, the goal projected by Austin evokes the spirit of the Cold War. As a reporter in the *New York Times* commented:

'Mr. Austin and others in the Biden administration are becoming more explicit about the future they see: years of continuous contest for power and influence with Moscow that in some ways resembles what President John F. Kennedy termed the "long twilight struggle" of the Cold War'[53].

One of the characteristic features of the condition of historical amnesia is the tendency to read history backwards. This failure to take seriously the legacy of the past leads to an inability to grasp the unique features of the contemporary era. It is the lack of respect for historical specificity that leads sections of the commentariat to represent Russia's invasion of Ukraine as the latest version of the old Cold War. The 'original Cold War's end was a mirage' wrote Stephen Kotkin in an article titled 'The Cold War Never Ended' in *Foreign Affairs*[54]. 'Some ex-

49 https://www.standard.co.uk/news/world/what-is-new-world-order-joe-biden-conspiracy-theorists-online-qanon-b990263.html
50 https://www.telegraph.co.uk/world-news/2022/03/02/joe-biden-makes-embarrassing-gaffe-saying-putin-will-never-win
51 https://www.washingtonpost.com/national-security/2022/04/16/us-nato-isolate-russia
52 https://www.nytimes.com/2022/04/25/us/politics/ukraine-russia-us-dynamic.html
53 https://www.nytimes.com/2022/04/25/us/politics/ukraine-russia-us-dynamic.html
54 https://www.foreignaffairs.com/reviews/review-essay/2022-04-06/cold-war-never-ended-russia-ukraine-war?check_logged_in=1

perts now view the current tensions as merely a new phase in a Cold War that never ended' reports Ronin Wright in the *New Yorker*.[55] Wright cites Sergey Radchenko, an international-relations expert at the School of Advanced International Studies at Johns Hopkins University, who asserts that the 'assumption in Washington that the Cold War was over in 1989 was "unduly American-centric" and ignored Moscow's historic desire to be seen and respected by the U.S. and Europe as a major power, regardless of ideology'[56].

'How quickly we have spun back up to Cold War like hostility' wrote the historian of the post-Cold War, Mary Elise Sarotte in the *New York Times*'[57]. Suddenly it has become painfully evident that the era between the end of the Cold War and the outbreak of the Covid pandemic was one marked by self-deception and historical amnesia. Contrary to conventional wisdom, the end of the Cold War did not mean the beginning of an era of permanent peace.

The use of the Cold War analogy to illuminate the chain of events unleashed by Russia's invasion of Ukraine fails to grasp current geopolitical realities. In particular, it overlooks what is the most alarming feature of this conflict, which is that it is actually a hot war and not a cold one! It is essential to recall that the Cold War suppressed military conflicts in Europe. The prospect of a nuclear war deterred both sides from directly attacking one another. That is why the historian John Lewis Gaddis characterised this period as the Long Peace[58]. Some even referred to the Cold War decades as *Pax Europaea*, European Peace[59]. At least for the European continent, the Cold War coincided with the most peaceful decades of the 20th century. The threat of nuclear annihilation deterred the two sides from attacking one another. The two dominant powers – the United States and the Soviet Union – suppressed conflicts between rivals on their side. In this way, traditional rivalries such as between Germany and France were subordinated to the global East-West confrontation. Compared to today, there was clarity about the rules governing international relations.

Unlike the current era, the global system during the decades of the Cold War was relatively stable. In contrast to the bipolar system that prevailed during the Cold War, today's multipolar world has not yet established the conditions for

55 https://www.newyorker.com/news/daily-comment/does-the-us-russia-crisis-over-ukraine-prove-that-the-cold-war-never-ended
56 https://www.newyorker.com/news/daily-comment/does-the-us-russia-crisis-over-ukraine-prove-that-the-cold-war-never-ended
57 https://www.nytimes.com/2022/03/01/opinion/russia-ukraine-cold-war.html
58 See Duffield, J.S. (1994) 'Explaining the Long Peace in Europe: the contributions of regional security regimes', *Review of International Studies*, vol. 20, no. 4.
59 https://www.college-de-france.fr/site/samantha-besson/guestlecturer-2022-10-19-17h00.htm

clarity about the balance of power. For a start, there are more major players with skin in the game than during the Cold War. American policymakers may fantasise about the glory days of Cold War superpower rivalry, but the world is no longer bipolar. There is China and India to consider. Nor are the other nations of Asia, the Middle East and Latin America likely to reconcile themselves to the role of bit players in the next phase of a global drama.

The most useful historical analogy that helps to make sense of the situation today is not the Cold War, but the years that led to the outbreak of the First World War. What characterised those years in the early part of the 20th century was the eruption of economic rivalry and political conflict. This was the moment when it was far from clear how the different sides would line up in the coming Great War. When the war broke out in 1914, Italy was still a partner in the Triple Alliance with Germany and Austria-Hungary but decided to stay neutral. It soon decided to jump ship and in May 1915 declared war against Austria-Hungary. After this flip-flop, the world had to wait until April 1917 before the United States finally decided to enter the fray and declare war on Germany.

If anything, the situation today is potentially even more complicated than in the early part of the 20th century. Washington may wish to isolate Russia, but any policy of containment will be tested by the response of China, India and other parts of the so-called developing world to its exercise of *realpolitik*. Nor can the unity of the West be taken for granted. The half-hearted response of Germany to demands for supporting the cause of Ukraine highlights the tensions within the West. In Germany, public opinion has become increasingly war-weary. According to a poll carried out on 28 April 2022, only 45 per cent of Germans supported the delivery of heavy weapons to Ukraine. This represented a 10-percentage point decline in support in a matter of weeks[60]. Similarly, significant sections of French and Italian society have lost much of their early enthusiasm for the war. Even in the United States opinion regarding providing military and financial aid to Ukraine is divided. The spirit of Cold War unity is conspicuously absent in many parts of the West.

Cold War Envy

The project of evoking the spirit of the Cold War is entirely understandable. Despite the threat of a nuclear war, the cause of standing up to the challenge posed

---

60 See https://www.euractiv.com/section/politics/news/public-opinion-crumbles-over-german-war-support-to-ukraine

by the Soviet Union endowed the West with great moral clarity. Many of the problems that haunted the societies of Europe in the first half of the 20th centu-ry-intense ideological conflict, economic upheaval, erosion of legitimacy-seemed to pale into insignificance in a global environment where the choice between good and evil was straightforward and self-evident to all. During this time cap-italism became re-legitimised, extreme ideologies were laid to rest and the inse-curity and economic anxieties of the interwar years were displaced by an era of unprecedented prosperity. At the time, the unexpected and at first unnoticed ar-rival of the Golden Age of Capitalism – from 1947 to 1973 – helped to steady the nerves.

That the end of the Cold War in 1991would turn out to be a mixed blessing was recognised at the time by astute observers. No sooner did the Cold War come to an end before a sense of nostalgia for the certainties and moral clarity provid-ed by a world divided between good and evil kicked in. The former diplomat and influential economist John K. Galbraith wrote that the 'hard intruding fact is that in the last 45 years, just short of a half-century, no one has been killed, accidents apart, in a conflict between the rich and relatively affluent industrial countries of the globe, this being true as between the capitalist ... and those which have char-acterised themselves as communist'. Galbraith's lament for the good old days of the Cold War were echoed in the *Financial Times:* the 'West's relief at ending the Cold War is history. It has been superseded by the fears of political instability and an awareness that integrating eastern Europe, not to mention the Soviet Union into the world economy poses difficulties of a hitherto unimagined com-plexity'[61]. As Russia's invasion of Ukraine indicates, concerns about the 'unima-gined complexity' of forging a *modus vivendi* with the old Soviet Union were well founded.

'Why We Will Soon Miss The Cold War', was the title of an influential essay written by the international relations scholar John J. Mearsheimer in *The Atlantic* in August 1990[62]. Arguably the most influential advocate of the realist school of international relations, Mearsheimer understood that the Cold War had merely suppressed and not resolved some of the conflicts that haunted the European continent in the previous era. He noted:

'We may, however, wake up one day lamenting the loss of the order that the Cold War gave to the anarchy of international relations. For untamed anarchy is what Europe knew in the forty-five years of this century before the Cold War, and untamed anarchy—Hobbes's war of

---

61 See Galbraith, J.K., 'The price of world peace', *The Guardian*, 8 September 1990, and *Financial Times*, 7 January 1991.

62 https://www.theatlantic.com/past/docs/politics/foreign/mearsh.htm

all against all—is a prime cause of armed conflict. Those who think that armed conflicts among the European states are now out of the question, that the two world wars burned all the war out of Europe, are projecting unwarranted optimism onto the future. The theories of peace that implicitly undergird this optimism are notably shallow constructs'.

Mearsheimer asserted that 'the prospect of major crises, even wars, in Europe is likely to increase dramatically now that the Cold War is receding into history'.

Mearsheimer drew attention to the potential for the eruption of global disorder in the aftermath of the end of the Cold War. However, the end of the Cold War also brought to the surface the moral and existential crisis that afflicted the West throughout the 20th century. As I explained in my study, *First World War: Still No End In Sight*, this conflict set in motion a chain of events which has been described as the Age of Catastrophe. Political polarisation in the interwar period tends to be interpreted through the prism of ideological struggles between the left and the right. However, the dramatic upsurge of radical ideological polarisation obscured an equally important development, which was the erosion of the norms and values that supported the taken-for-granted practices that defined life before the war. As one American historian pointed out 'the First World War had a dissolvent effect upon conventional belief and behaviour'[63].

One of the most momentous and durable legacies of the Great War was that it disrupted and disorganised the prevailing web of meaning through which Western societies made sense of their world. Suddenly the key values and ideals into which the early 20th century elites were socialised appeared to be emptied of meaning. 'Europe was exhausted, not just physically, but also morally' wrote Jan-Werner Müller in his study of the 'crisis of confidence among European elites after the war'[64].

Cold War Stability

Although periodically the Cold War appeared as a direct prelude to World War III and at times threatened to turn into a frightening confrontation between the major nuclear powers, its impact on global affairs was a conservative one. Paradoxically the Cold War worked to stabilise the global order. Cold War anxieties created a demand for security and in such circumstances, the maintenance of the status quo was held to be a value in and of itself.

---

63 See http://www.nytimes.com/books/first/h/himmelfarb-cultures.html
64 Müller, J.-W. (2013) *Contesting Democracy: Political Ideas In Twentieth Century Europe*, Yale University Press: New Haven, p. 24.

As it turned out, the Cold War provided both sides – but especially the West – with a focus for unity. During this time, domestic divisions could be suppressed by the intensity of a highly charged conflict between superpowers. The Cold War provided both sides with a clearly identifiable external enemy. At the same time, given the ideological dimension of the rivalry between the two superpowers, the conflict also assumed a domestic dimension. Fear of the Soviet threat was paralleled by apprehension towards its domestic radical and communist allies. The threat of communism served as a focus for unity amongst otherwise disparate parties of social democrats, of the centre and of the right. In some Western societies – particularly in the United State – anticommunism acquired a powerful momentum and served the role of a quasi-ideology. Hostility towards the menace of communism provided Western governments with an opportunity to avoid facing up to their own intellectual and moral deficiencies. The contrast with the Soviet Union worked to the benefit of Western societies and helped them gain the moral high ground without having to provide a compelling account of themselves.

Unlike the 1930s when Soviet industrialisation caught the imagination of millions of people suffering under mass unemployment in the capitalist world, by the 1950s it was the West that was seen as dynamic and capable of improving living standards. Indeed, by the 1960s, the internal flaws of the Soviet economy had become increasingly perceived as a model to be avoided.

During the Cold War the advocates of Western capitalism sought to consolidate their position by counterposing their way of life against Communism. By the time of the outbreak of the Korean War in June 1950, it was evident that anxiety about the intention of the Stalinist bloc was spreading rapidly among intellectuals and opinion-makers in Western societies. The negative example of the Soviet Union helped anticommunism gain influence. It also provided Western governments with their most powerful ideological weapon for enhancing their authority. However, in the long run, the negative worldview of anticommunism lacked the moral and intellectual depth required to legitimate a particular way of life. The failure to construct a positive worldview based on the affirmation of the virtues of liberal democracy would be exposed in the late 1960s and continues to haunt society today.

In retrospect, it is evident that the Cold War provided a provisional solution to the moral crisis of the West. This was the moment where the West could claim that it stood for something. During the Cold War, the construction of a way of life – at least in the West – was facilitated by the ominous presence of a negative despotic model. For decades, the Soviet threat, which served as the symbol of evil, provided Western societies with an opportunity to justify – at least negatively – their way of life. President Ronald Reagan's Evil Empire speech on 8 March

1983 was not simply a denunciation of the Soviet Union but the affirmation of the American way of life:

> 'Yes, let us pray for the salvation of all of those who live in that totalitarian darkness—pray they will discover the joy of knowing God. But until they do, let us be aware that while they preach the supremacy of the state, declare its omnipotence over individual man, and predict its eventual domination of all peoples on the Earth, they are the focus of evil in the modern world' [65].

This speech, which was made to a group of evangelical Christians may have been deliberately given in a quasi-religious tone. But it reached beyond its audience to provide a powerful illustration of the way that Cold War ideology could be used as an instrument for the moralisation of the American way of life.

During the era of superpower rivalries, moral uncertainty and the problem of legitimacy could by be displaced by highlighting the threat posed by the Evil Empire. However, the suspension of the Cold War rivalries in the late 1980s brought to the fore problems of legitimacy that were previously obscured by the intensity of highly ideological superpower conflicts.

It was as if the end of the Cold War had robbed the West of any real meaning As one contributor to a 1990 *Foreign Affairs* discussion on the post-Cold War global order put it, a 'plausible vision of the common good remains stubbornly elusive'[66]. The American historian William McNeill linked his concern about the absence of a common good to the difficulty of forging a domestic consensus, which could 'even imperil constitutional procedures'. Concern about domestic consensus focused on social cohesion and moral values. As far as McNeill was concerned, the Cold War served to displace anxieties about domestic matters and relocate them onto the plane of foreign affairs. He noted that 'unless some new foreign danger raises its head, American politicians and the public will have to think about what ought to happen at home[67].

Across the Atlantic, the English military historian Michael Howard was prescient when he observed that the long-term challenge facing the West was that of 'maintaining cohesion in increasingly heterogenous societies'. He observed that social tensions and mass immigration have 'eroded the cultural cohesion of older communities'[68]. Howard concluded that 'we are left with a West whose wealth provides no relief from anxiety and turbulence'. The problem of legitima-

---

65 For the text of this speech, see http://www.reaganfoundation.org/bw_detail.aspx?p= LMB4YGHF2&h1=0&h2=0&sw=&lm=berlinwall&args_a=cms&args_b=74&argsb=N&tx=1770
66 McNeill, W.H. (1989) 'Winds of change', *Foreign Affairs.*, vol. 69, p. 161.
67 *Ibid.*
68 Howard, M. (1991) *The Lessons of History*, Clarendon Press: Oxford, p. 4.

cy, which Howard characterised as the absence of 'cultural cohesion', has re-
mained a constant source of anxiety to this day.

In hindsight, it appears that Cold War certainties relieved the West of the
burden of having to confront the moral malaise that lurked in the background.
In the aftermath of the Cold War, the consequence of the moral impasse could no
longer be evaded. It was as if the West stood morally depleted. The American author William Pfaff wrote in his *Barbarian Sentiments: How the American Century
Ends*, that there is no longer an intellectually responsible ruling idea of Ameri-
canism, a fully acceptable formulation of this justificatory national purpose—
to say nothing of a national policy to advance it'. He added that 'there 'no longer
is a clear ethnic identity'[69].

A consciousness of a moral impasse amongst sections of the Western elite
created the condition where, almost imperceptibly, their focus of attention drift-
ed from the Cold War to the Culture War. In his 'A Conservative Research Agenda
for the 90s', Adam Myerson, editor of the American publication, *Policy Review*
warned, 'as Communism collapses, the greatest ideological threat to western civ-
ilization—now comes from within the West's own cultural institutions—the universities, the churches, the professions such as law and medicine, and above all
the disintegrating family'[70]. The taken-for-granted unity that prevailed during the
Cold War gave way to divisions and cultural conflicts over values.

One of the unexpected outcomes of the end of the Cold War was that it deprived Western governments of one of the most effective instruments of valida-
tion. That is why time and again politicians and policymakers have acknowledged their nostalgia for the certainties of the Cold War years. As Dick
Cheney, the former vice-president of the U.S. recalled in February 2002, 'when
America's great enemy suddenly disappeared, many wondered what new direction our foreign policy would take'[71]. Confusion about the future direction of foreign policy was by no means the only outcome of the demise of the Cold War. A
similar pattern of disorientation is also evident in relation to domestic affairs.

One reason why the defeat of the Soviet Union did not lead to the strengthening of the normative foundation of liberal democracies was that the West had
done very little to develop a positive account of this doctrine throughout the Cold
War. Aside from the rhetoric of freedom versus enslavement and good versus
evil, the West was almost entirely dependent on the appeal of its economic success during its global confrontation with the communist world. As Karl Dietrich

---

69 Pfaff, W. (1990) *Barbarian Sentiments: How the American Century Ends*, The Noonday Press:
New York, p. 185.
70 Meyerson, A. (1990) 'The Vision Thing Continued', *Policy Review*, p. 2.
71 Text of speech is available on https://www.mtholyoke.edu/acad/intrel/bush/cheneyiraq.htm

Bracher explained during the Cold War, the idea of freedom was attractive but 'previously unknown prosperity' helped and its appeal was 'made more conspicuous by contrast with the repulsive picture of communist coercive rule and coercive economy'. He added that, at this time, attempts to develop 'a philosophical and moral foundation of libertarian-democratic policies were lagging behind a pragmatic orientation'[72]. In other words, people were drawn toward the Western way of life during the Cold War mainly because of its economic superiority and its promise of prosperity. Consequently, it was not enthusiastic approval but self-interested pragmatism that underpinned the calculation of citizens on both sides of the East-West divide. The appeal of the West, both to those who lived in it and to those who wanted to live in it, was a better way of life. But that 'better way of life' was largely perceived as a better standard of economic life that was not necessarily connected to ideology.

After the end of the Cold War, Western governments could no longer rely on the legacy of economic efficiency and prosperity to spare them the responsibility of validating their way of life in the language of politics and culture. In the long run, capitalist efficiency and productivity does not provide a sufficient basis for moral authority. In any case, by the 1990s, the post-war boom had given way to economic insecurity and instability.

By the turn of the 21st century, it was evident that the triumph of the West in the Cold War was as much to do with the negative contrast provided by the Soviet Union as with a capacity to inspire people with a positive vision of a good life. The Soviet Union and the official communist movement more or less gave up the ghost. The Soviet bloc had for a long time sought to distance itself from its traditional beliefs and by the 1980s it had to some extent acknowledged the irrelevance of its ideology. The subsequent implosion of the Soviet Union and of the political movements inspired by the traditions of the Bolshevik Revolution of October 1917 were as much a result of loss of belief and an act of self-destruction as of a defeat on the battlefield of ideas. Indeed, at times it appeared that the leaders of the official communist movement were far more committed to burying their ideological heritage than to preserving it. As the French historian François Furet indicated, 'former Communists seem obsessed with the negation of the regime in which they lived'[73].

The most significant outcome of the disintegration of the Soviet bloc and of the communist movement was that it strengthened the view that there was no alternative to the capitalist market. Former opponents of capitalism drew the

---

72 Bracher, K.D. (1984) *The Age of Ideologies*, Weidenfeld and Nicholson: London, p. 194.
73 Furet, F. (1990) 'From 1789 to 1917–1989', *Encounter*, September, p. vii.

conclusion that this system was the most efficient regulator of economic life and by the 1980s the critics of the market were far weaker and more defensive than at any time in the 20th century.

Francis Fukuyama, who responded to the end of the Cold War with his claim that history had ended, found it easier to explain the success of the capitalist economic system than the 'victory of liberal democracy in the political sphere'[74]. Indeed, he found it difficult to provide a compelling account of democracy's alleged triumph. On the contrary, he suggested democratic values on their own lack the power to inspire and therefore require that citizens establish some form of emotional identification with their system. He concluded that 'they must come to love democracy not because it is necessarily better than the alternatives, but because it is *theirs*'[75].

One of the most important insights that Fukuyama offered in his *End of History* was that liberalism in its classical form contained insufficient moral content to provide guidance to people and to provide a normative foundation for authority. He explained that 'beyond establishing rules for mutual self-preservation, liberal societies do not attempt to define any positive goals for their citizens or promote a particular way of life as superior or desirable to another'[76]. If indeed liberal democracy avoided the question of normativity and sought to bypass the challenge of arguing for a version of moral norms, it would be in serious trouble. Contrary to Fukuyama's thesis, there would certainly not be an end of history. No society – liberal or otherwise – can evade the challenge of providing norms and ideals for guiding people's lives and for validating itself. Security, efficiency and material well-being are indispensable for community life but on their own is insufficient for its flourishing.

European Union's Post-Cold War Predicament

A growing awareness of the problem of legitimacy became a major issue for the leaders of the European Union in the post-Cold War years. It is important to note that since the end of the Second World War, the supporters of European federalism have always been concerned about the weakness of the value-based foundation on which their project rested. From the 1950s onwards, the advocates of European integration and unification have tended to be more comfortable about

---

74 Fukuyama (1992) *The End of History and the Last Man*, Free Press: New York pp. 90–91.
75 Fukuyama (1992), p. 215.
76 Fukuyama (1992), p. 160.

promoting an economic justification for their cause than in attempting to win support for an explicit system of shared values. Throughout its history, the project of European unification gained respect and support for the economic, and to a lesser extent, the geo-political advantages that it offered. Institutions like the old European Economic Community (EEC) took the credit for the improved material conditions of Western European societies and, throughout the 1960s, its moral authority was rarely discussed, let alone tested.

The problem of providing a normative foundation for the European project was evident to many leading advocates of the European federalist project. Their response in the 1950s and '60s was to avoid an explicit engagement with the domain of values. Instead, they opted to sidestep this issue by attempting to evade dealing overtly with the question of values. Instead, the main arguments for European unification stressed its contribution to the promotion of economic prosperity and the provision of security in the face of the Cold War. Until the 1970s, the viability of this approach was underwritten by the post-war boom, an unprecedented era of economic prosperity.

European transnational institutions were in themselves also the progeny of the Cold War. The heightened geopolitical tension during the Cold War in the 1950s and '60s helped strengthen the claim of the EEC that it was essential for the maintenance of security. The launching of the European Union in 1993 continued a tradition of depoliticising values and related issues and adopting a form of technocratic governance that relied on the claim that it played a vital role in the maintenance of economic prosperity.

In the context of the Cold War and of relative economic security, the project of European unification faced relatively little pressure to justify itself in normative terms. Consequently, the capacity of its normative power to influence developments was rarely tested. Until the mid-1970s the leaders of the EEC adhered to the conviction that the benefits of economic co-operation would eventually encourage the people of the continent to politically identify with the European project.

However, in the 1970s, advocates of the European project realised that reliance on economics alone was not enough; the formulation of a normative foundation on which the authority of their institution rested had to be addressed. Their calls for a 'new narrative for Europe' were motivated by the realisation that the EU could no longer count on the Cold War to indefinitely legitimise its standing. Nor could it forever rely on the stabilising influence of economic prosperity to retain the passive support of the public for its institutions.

The linking of the fortunes of the project of European Unity with economic stability and the wellbeing of the continent became increasingly problematic from 1973 onwards. The economic crisis of 1973 indicated to the leadership of the EEC that it was necessary to find an explicitly political or cultural justification for its existence. The leadership of the EEC responded by attempting to mobilise the resources of culture in an effort to win hearts and minds[77].

Since the 1970s, a series of recurrent economic crises has forced the EU to try to supplement its economic authority with a series of cultural initiatives. The October 2004 EU-sponsored report, *The Spiritual and Cultural Dimension of Europe*, recognised that, with the end of the Cold War, economics must continue to play an important role in legitimating the authority of the EU. Its 'Concluding Remarks' penned by Kurt Biedenkopf, Bronislaw Geremek and Krzysztof Michalski stated:

> As memories of the Second World War faded and the risk of conflict between the Atlantic Alliance and the Soviet Union receded, the transformation of the EEC into the European Community, and finally into the European Union, pushed the Union's economic goals ever more to the fore. Economic growth, improvement in living standards, extending and enhancing systems of social protection, and rounding off the common market assumed a priority'[78].

However, although this report emphasised the importance of economic growth for underwriting the authority of the EU, it also recognised that something else was needed to endow this institution with legitimacy.

The report concluded that the principal challenge facing the EU was a political one and that therefore the viability of the project of unification depended on its ability to establish a political foundation for its authority. It warned that the 'internal cohesion that is necessary for the European Union' cannot be provided by 'economic forces alone':

> 'It is no coincidence that economic integration is not enough to drive European political reform. Economic integration simply does not, of itself, lead to political integration because **markets cannot produce a politically resilient solidarity** (emphasis added). Solidarity— a genuine sense of civic community—is vital because the competition that dominates the marketplace gives rise to powerful centrifugal forces. Markets may create the economic basis of a polity and are thereby an indispensable condition of its political constitution. But they cannot on their own produce political integration and provide a constitutive infra-

---

77 See Kaiser, W. (2015) 'Clash of Cultures: Two Milieus in the European Union—A New Narrative For Europe Project', *Journal of Contemporary European Studies*, vol. 12, no. 3 p. 374.
78 https://ec.europa.eu/research/social-sciences/pdf/other_pubs/michalski_091104_report_an nexes_en.pdf

structure for the Union. The original expectation, that the political unity of the EU would be a consequence of the European common market has proven to be illusory'[79].

In pointing out the limits of economics for maintaining and developing the political unity of the EU, the authors of this report echoed the pithy statement made previously by Jacques Delors, former president of the European Commission, who noted in his essay, *Our Europe*, that 'nobody falls in love with a growth rate'.

A report published by the EU in 2013 – *New Narrative For Europe* and the publication *Mind And Body Of Europe: New Narrative* – explicitly recognized that the end of the Cold War represented a challenge to the standing and relevance of the EU. The Luxembourg MEP and prominent advocate of the EU, Viviane Reding stated in *Mind And Body Of Europe: New Narrative* that:

> 'In recent years, the experiences of war, of totalitarian regimes and the Cold War have gradually lost their immediacy in the eyes of the general public, which is to say that those horrors are losing their legitimising force. More and more Europeans regard the experiences of the 20th century—rightly or wrongly—*as a thing of the past* [emphasis added][80].

The call for a new narrative for European unity was motivated by the understanding that, in the post-Cold War era, the EU could no longer rely on the passive acquiescence of the European public. The authors of the report understood that historical amnesia may mean that people regard the experiences of the 20th century simply 'as a thing of the past' and that indifference to the past would deprive the EU of a legitimating focus.

A Crisis of Meaning

For all its limitations, Cold War ideology at least provided policymakers and society with an explanatory framework for interpreting global events. Its loss, which led to the rapid disintegration of assumptions, conventions and practices associated with the Cold War order, has led to what Zaki Laïdi has characterised as a 'world crisis of meaning'[81]. This crisis of meaning is the outcome of the in-

---

79 https://ec.europa.eu/research/social-sciences/pdf/other_pubs/michalski_091104_report_annexes_en.pdf

80 Reding, V. (2013) 'Stimulating the European Public Space', *Mind And Body Of Europe: New Narrative*, p. 32.

81 Laïdi, Z. (1998) *A World Without Meaning: The Crisis Of Meaning In International Politics*, Routledge: London, p. 16.

capacity of public institutions and conventions to provide clarity of purpose for the conduct of policy. The absence of a vision of a common good was most strikingly demonstrated by the continuing decline of 'public confidence in the performance of representative institutions in Western Europe, North America and Japan'[82]. The post-Cold War 'feel-good' factor soon gave way to a new era of mistrust and alienation from public life.

Since the turn of the 21st century, the Western political establishment had sought to contain the damage caused by domestic cultural conflict by gaining moral clarity through its foreign policy. Not long after the destruction of the World Trade Center by a terrorist attack on 11 September 2001, the former American Secretary for Education William Bennett published a fascinating testimony that seamlessly made a conceptual leap from the Cold War to the Culture War and then landed in the middle of a new War on Terror His book titled, *Why We Fight: Moral Clarity And The War On Terrorism* is as open as it is naïve about its hope in gaining meaning and a sense of belonging through the war on terror. He declared:

> 'And what a wonderful, heart swelling surprise *that* was, especially to those of us, veterans of the "culture war" of the last three or four decades, who had kept an alarmed watch over the hardening of divisions among us and the downward course of our country's cultural indicators. ... There were moments during those years when even the basic, taken for granted unity of the US, in anything more than a rhetorical sense, was beginning to seem in doubt. But the events of September 11, and the amazing response to them, had killed all such doubts'[83].

Here a 'veteran' of the decades-long culture wars paused to revel in the 'wonderful, heart swelling surprise' that, when confronted with a brutal act of terror, the nation is united after all. Bennett had little doubt that this unexpected unity of his nation was gained through the war. The question posed in his book's title – *Why We Fight* – invited the obvious answer: because of the moral clarity gained through it.

It is evident that Bennett, along with many of his colleagues, regarded the so-called War on Terror as an opportunity to relive the Cold War and experience the sense of national unity created by a global environment where the choice between good and evil was straightforward and self-evident to all. That, at the turn of the 21st century, war could serve as the source of moral rehabilitation, explains

---

82 See Pharr, S. J., Putnam, R. D. and Dalton, Russell J. (2000) 'A Quarter-Century of Declining Confidence', *Journal of Democracy*, vol. 11, no. 2, p. 9.
83 Bennett, W.J. (2003) *Why We Fight. Moral Clarity and the War on Terrorism*, Regnery Publishing Inc: Washington, D.C. p. 145.

the Cold War envy that has been evoked by the conflict in Ukraine. For many policy makers, the public's reaction to Russia's invasion of Ukraine also represented a 'wonderful, heart swelling surprise'.

One symptom of the post-Cold War malaise is the inability of Western societies to replicate the consensus and unity of that era. The problem of galvanising public support around a common objective became evident to policymakers in the years that followed the War on Terror. One study of British public diplomacy concluded that it is far more difficult to convince citizens to back the official line on the War on Terror than it was to back the Cold War[84]. This loss of Cold War certainty was coupled with the awareness that society's capacity to integrate its citizens had become seriously compromised. So, a study published in 2008 about the security threat facing Britain reported that 'we are in a confused and vulnerable condition'. It indicated that one reason for this sense of insecurity was because 'we lack the certainty of the old rigid geometry' of the Cold War[85]. Confronted by what it perceived as the 'loss of confidence' and the absence of an overarching moral purpose in British society, the authors could not but mourn the loss of the Cold War.

This acknowledgement of the loss of Cold War certainty and the consequent emergence of a sense of vulnerability was directly equated to the conditions that led up to the outbreak of World War One. The authors argued that the 'stiff geometry of the Cold War world has given way to a less predictable (although actually older and familiar) flow of forces in world affairs'. The 'older and familiar' global dynamic it referred to was that of the early years of the 20th century. Pointing to the absence of social cohesion and agreement about fundamental values it stated that 'in all three ways – our social fragmentation, the sense of premonition and the divisions about what our stance should be – there are uneasy similarities with the years just before the First World War'[86]

This prescient report, published in 2008, provides a useful context for understanding the project of framing the current conflict in Ukraine as Cold War 2.0. Unfortunately, the quest for legitimacy by the West may well lead to outcomes that may contradict the interests of the people of Ukraine.

---

84 See Leonard, M., Small, A. and Rose, M. (2005) *British Public Diplomacy in the "Age of Schisms"*, The Foreign Policy Centre: London, p. 11.

85 Prins, G. and Salisbury, R. (2008) *Risk, Threat and Security; The case of the United Kingdom*, RUSI: London, p. 4.

86 Prins & Salisbury (2008), p. 3.

Chapter 3
Ukraine and the Enduring Salience of Nationhood

The war in the Ukraine has called on us to reflect on the many discussions about globalism and nationalism, stability and conflict, and unity and borders. Questions that claimed attention during the COVID pandemic about the nature of national divisions and co-operations, of borders and economic phenomena, and the embrace of cosmopolitan ideology seem to have re-emerged through discussions of war. The political, economic and ideological landscapes are changing.

A BBC reporter explaining why Finland is just about to join NATO is interviewing a reservist, who informs us that an unprecedented number of young people are signing up to join the army. One young reservist explains that he joined because 'we need to have a credible military' to deter the Russians. He explains that his message to Russia is 'you keep on your side of the border, and we will keep on ours'[87]. He, along with millions of other Finns, are in no doubt that borders really matter. His experience directly calls into question the fashionable cause of 'open borders'. It was precisely because millions of Ukrainians took the defence of their borders so seriously that the Russian invaders failed to achieve their strategic objectives.

Military commentators and experts throughout the world had little doubt that, once Russia invaded Ukraine, the war would be over in a couple of weeks if not days. They all expected a 'quick Russian battlefield victory'[88]. For example, shortly before Russia's invasion, the American Chairman of the Joint Chiefs of Staff, General Mark Milley, informed congressional leaders during a private meeting that Ukraine would 'fall in 72 hours'[89]. Milley's sentiments were widely shared by Western officials on both sides of the Atlantic. When the Ukrainian ambassador to Germany asked for help, his request was politely rejected on the ground that it was pointless to send weapons since the war would be over in 48 hours[90].

No doubt there are many reasons why Russia's war plan failed to realise its objectives. Numerous commentators have drawn attention to the disorganised state of its army, its tactical ineptitude and low morale. However, whatever the limitations and defects of Russia's military strategy, the most important reason

---

87 *Today Programme*, BBC Radio 4, 12 May 2002.

88 https://www.nytimes.com/2022/04/28/opinion/russia-ukraine-biden-aid.html

89 https://www.heritage.org/defense/commentary/why-gen-milleys-ukraine-war-prediction-missed-mile

90 https://www.gisreportsonline.com/r/russian-military-power

https://doi.org/10.1515/9783110981544-005

for its swift unravelling was the unexpected resistance of the people of Ukraine. As one BBC reporter noted, 'Ukrainian willingness to fight and die upended every prediction of a swift Russian victory'[91]. That so many Western observers did not anticipate the willingness of so many Ukrainians to fight is not surprising since prevailing attitudes in their society tend to eschew the 'readiness to sacrifice one's life'[92]. Research on attitudes and values in Western societies suggests that readiness to sacrifice one's life has given way to an increasing insistence on 'living it, and living it the way one chooses'[93].

In their study of the phenomenon of declining willingness to fight for one's country, Ronald Inglehart, Bi Puranen and Christine Welzel argue that 'ascending life opportunities give rise to pro-choice values', a condition that is the main driver of this phenomenon. They conclude that 'as these values become widespread, people's willingness to fight other countries dwindles'[94]. From this perspective, it seems that one of the outcomes of rising prosperity and stability is a diminishing sense of duty, patriotism, and altruistic sacrifice. In contrast, I would argue that it is not so much prosperity and pro-choice values but the tendency towards the cultural devaluation of national attachments, patriotism, duty and service that may influence individuals' willingness to fight in a war. National attachments and the willingness to defend one's community need not be undermined by prosperity. As I argue elsewhere, the aversion to losing and risk-taking in Western societies are underpinned by a sense of cultural disorientation rather than prosperity[95]. There are, of course, numerous variables that explain national differences such as between Finland, where 74 per cent of those surveyed indicated that they were prepared to fight, as opposed to Holland, where only 15 per cent indicated that they were prepared to go to war for their country[96]. Finns have a far stronger sense of belonging to a national community than their Dutch peers. Their willingness to fight is in part due to their strong attachment to their way of life and community.

---

91 https://www.bbc.co.uk/news/world-europe-61027292

92 Inglehart, R.F., Puranen, B. and Welzel, C. (2015) 'Declining willingness to fight for one's country: The individual-level basis of the long peace', *Journal of Peace Research*, vol. 52, no. 4, pp. 418–434.

93 *Ibid.* p. 432.

94 *Ibid.* p. 432.

95 See Furedi, F. (2007) *Invitation To Terror; The Expanding Empire Of The Unknown*, Bloomsbury: London.

96 See results from the 2015 WIN/Gallup International global survey, http://gallup-international.bg/en/Publications/2015/220-WIN-Gallup-International%E2%80%99s-global-survey-shows-three-in-five-willing-to-fight-for-their-country, and https://brilliantmaps.com/europe-fight-war.

The key reason why so many Western observers did not expect Ukraine to withstand the Russian onslaught of their homeland is rooted in their underestimation of the significance that people tend to attach to their homeland. In recent decades – but especially since Russia invaded Ukraine and seized Crimea in 2014 – people's sense of nationhood has solidified remarkably. National attachment and identity do not merely pertain to the domain of values and attitudes. They rest on Place and are underpinned by a sensibility that is organically linked to a community and its forms of being. 'Ukrainians see their existence in time and space as resting on this vision of a sovereign history, emancipated from Russia', notes Georgiy Kasianov[97]. Kasianov's emphasis on a national consciousness and sovereign history is important for understanding the strength of feeling and determination displayed by the men and women fighting for Ukraine's independence. In a recently published survey designed to explain who amongst the Ukrainian population is willing to fight and what motivated their decision to take up arms, Pippa Norris and Kseniya Kizilova note that 'feelings of Ukrainian pride and self-identified closeness to the country were indeed positive predictors of willingness for military service, while Russophone populations were more reluctant to join up'[98].

Norris and Kizilova also emphasise that individuals' endorsement of democratic values also motivated people to resist Russia's invasion. They note that 'the forces of nationalism are strong but appeals to democratic freedoms also appear to contribute towards the mobilisation of citizen soldiers'. The authors' counterposition of the forces of nationalism and appeals to democratic freedom is likely to be influenced by a mistaken view that perceives nationalism as the antithesis of democracy. Rather, the sense of pride in nationhood is often intertwined with the aspiration for freedom and democracy. These sentiments were enshrined in the 18th century, post-revolutionary constitutions of France and the United States. In more recent times they have been expressed through a commitment to national independence and democracy and informed the different movements demanding the end of Soviet domination over their nations.

Norris and Kizilova's polarised representation of democracy and patriotism is widely shared amongst members of the Western academic community. It is underpinned by the conviction that national attachments possess no positive attributes. More broadly in the Western world, nationalism tends to be represented as an out-of-date and irrational outlook without any redeeming features. Aca-

97 https://www.foreignaffairs.com/articles/ukraine/2022-05-04/war-over-ukrainian-identi ty#author-info
98 https://blogs.lse.ac.uk/europpblog/2022/03/03/what-mobilises-the-ukrainian-resistance

demic commentators frequently assume that thankfully, in the contemporary globalised world, national attachments have lost much of their force. They believe that only fundamentalist movements of backward-looking populists are likely to be moved by nationalist concerns. No doubt in Europe in the 21st century, national identity competes with other forms of identity, but, as events in Ukraine indicate, it retains a powerful capacity to motivate people to fight for their country.

It is historical amnesia toward the legacy of the past that has lowered Western's experts' expectations of Ukraine's willingness to resist Russia's invasion of their society. The Western cultural establishment tends to regard patriotism as an old-fashioned prejudice; a historical legacy that the world can well do without. Typically, its attitude of estrangement towards the value of national sovereignty has meant that many Western commentators have felt the need to justify their support of Ukraine on the grounds that people were fighting for their democratic freedoms rather than for national sovereignty.

Globalisation and the Return of the Nation State

The war in Ukraine coincides with what's likely to be the final chapter in the demise of the ideology of globalisation. It is difficult to sustain this ideology in the face of current geopolitical realities. The geopolitical fallout from Russia's invasion of Ukraine has forced even the most ardent globalist to realise that the world is fast becoming divided into hostile economic blocks. This point was clearly recognised by the political and economic leaders who gathered at the May 2022 meeting of the World Economic Forum (WEF) in Davos. For decades, the powerful international players attending the WEF had praised the cosmopolitan ideals associated with the ideology of globalisation. By the time this meeting was held, it was evident that this ideology was running on empty. As one well-known globalist attending the event, José Manuel Barroso, chair of Goldman Sachs International and a former president of the European Commission, pointed out, 'tension between the US and China was accelerated by the pandemic and now this invasion of Ukraine by Russia—all these trends are raising serious concerns about a decoupling world.[99]'

The concept of globalisation highlights the trend towards the integration and internationalisation of the different parts of the world. Claims about the significance of this trend focus on the opening of the world to flows of capital, in-

---

99 https://www.ft.com/content/0599878e-a820-4657-8e52-f069bb10d512

vestment, trade and services. They stress the growing movement of people and the exchange of ideas. Communication flows of cultural symbols and practices are often depicted as evidence of the crystallisation of a global culture. For many globalist-minded individuals, globalisation represented a coming together of different parts of the world for the mutual benefit of all. It was frequently claimed that economic interaction would lead to the diminishing of political conflict. In the case of Germany, this naïve sentiment was expressed in the maxim of '*Wandel durch Handel*' – change through trade. Advocates of this maxim assumed that trade would push Russia and China towards adopting a freer, more democratic political system. They believed that with so much at stake in maintaining economic co-operation, Russia would be deterred from adopting an aggressive militaristic stance towards her Western partners. This sentiment was not only naïve but also self-serving. It served as a justification for allowing economic calculations to trump political ones. It was in this vein that George Osborne, the former British Conservative Chancellor of the Exchequer, could tell his Chinese audience at the Shanghai Stock Exchange in 2015, 'Let's stick together and make a golden era for the UK-China relationship'[100].

A lack of historical consciousness that underpins geopolitical naivety is particularly striking amongst members of the EU's political leadership. In March 2022, the former President of the European Commission, Jean-Claude Juncker, was forced to acknowledge this point. He told a roundtable discussion on the war in Ukraine that 'we were generally naïve'. He added that he is 'disappointed' in Vladimir Putin, with whom he had many discussions over the decades. In a tone of disappointment, he noted that 'this is not the Putin I have come to know in over 20 years'[101]. He added that 'all of us' did not imagine that Putin would attack Ukraine like he did.

Juncker and his colleagues should have been alert to the geopolitical realities confronting Europe as the phenomenon of globalisation was undermined by important events a long time before Russia invaded Ukraine. The viability of an open global economy was called into question by its disruption in the wake of the financial crisis of 2008. After the UK's vote to leave the EU in 2016 and the election of President Trump later that year, numerous observers concluded that globalisation was truly in crisis. Similar sentiments were expressed during the Covid Pandemic. In *Aftershocks: Pandemic Politics and the End of the Old International Order*, Colin Kahl and Thomas Wright claim that the pandemic accel-

---

100 https://www.gov.uk/government/speeches/chancellor-lets-create-a-golden-decade-for-the-uk-china-relationship
101 https://today.rtl.lu/news/luxembourg/a/1874924.html

erated pre-existing trends that have led to the breakdown of the American-led global order. During the pandemic, national competition for access to vaccines and medical equipment indicated that people throughout the world regarded the pursuit of national interest as a more effective way of protecting their health than merely relying on global competition. Hopes invested in transnational inter-dependence in security, economics, public health and the environment gave way to inter-state rivalry. The most dangerous example was the eruption of the U.S.-China trade war.[102]

That globalisation exhausted itself was indicated by the fact that the integra-tion of different parts of the world had been slowing for some time. Global cap-italism has still not recovered from the 2008 financial crisis when war broke out between Russia and Ukraine. Between 2008 and 2019, world trade relative to global G.D.P fell by 5 per cent[103]. According to research carried out by the Inter-national Monetary Fund, 'uncertainty around trade policies alone reduced global domestic product in 2019 by nearly 1 per cent'[104].

Since the crash of 2008–9, the fragility of the global financial system and global economic order has become all too evident. Between 2008 and 2018, glob-al trade growth had decreased by half compared with the previous decade[105]. Since the massive disruption caused by the Covid pandemic, the trends that came to the surface in 2008 have been impossible to ignore. The global supply chain crisis exacerbated by the economic slowdown due to the pandemic has, as the American economist Matt Stoller pointed out, 'left us uniquely unprepared to manage a supply shock'[106]. Globalisation proved singularly unprepared to deal with the crisis, and as Gerard Baker – the former editor-in-chief of the *Wall Street Journal* – argued it is likely to be Covid's greatest casualty[107].

These trends ran in parallel with the growth of economic nationalism. Phil Mullan has drawn attention to a report published by the World Trade Organisa-tion in June 2020, which 'shows that at the time of the 2008 financial crisis, fewer than one per cent of merchandise imports were impeded by mechanisms intro-

102 Kahl, C. & Wright, T. (2021) *Aftershocks: Pandemic Politics and the End of the Old Interna-tional Order*, St Martin's Press: New York.

103 https://www.economist.com/finance-and-economics/2022/03/19/globalisation-and-autoc racy-are-locked-together-for-how-much-longer

104 https://www.telegraph.co.uk/business/2022/05/22/economic-gloom-will-worsen-ukraine-war-causes-globalisation

105 Reinhart, C. and Reinhart, V. (2020) 'The pandemic depression: The global economy will never be the same', *Foreign Affairs*, vol. 99, p. 84.

106 https://www.theguardian.com/commentisfree/2021/oct/01/america-supply-chain-shortages

107 https://www.thetimes.co.uk/article/covids-biggest-scalp-will-be-globalisation-p7 m8rxkn7

duced by governments of the world's top 20 economies. In 2019, on the eve of the pandemic, this figure had expanded more than tenfold to hit over 10 per cent of world trade[108]. Economic protectionism – which in the past led to political and sometimes even military conflict – had made a comeback.

During the pandemic, national rivalries acquired momentum through the global scramble for access to pharmaceutical products, particularly vaccines. Supporters of the ideology of globalisation were taken aback by the sudden eruption of what came to be known as vaccine nationalism. Listing what it called 'disturbing factors', one account drew attention to 'attacks on global organisations such as the World Health Organization; the conflict between states over pharmaceutical tools and the support of medical research companies; and the de facto absence of leadership from international organisations like the European Union or G20 in response to this crisis'[109]. Similar warnings were issued in the *Harvard Business Review* about the 'Trump administration's acrimonious withdrawal from the World Health Organization at the height of the Covid-19 pandemic and the broader phenomenon of "vaccine nationalism", whereby states have sought national advantage through control over vaccine manufacture and distribution, have been particularly stark expressions of the conflict between nation-state organization and the globality of the human species woven together through myriad communication, technological, economic, and cultural networks'[110].

The vaccine nationalism that erupted during the pandemic reinforced the pre-existing trend toward the disruption of the institutions and conventions associated with the American-dominated international order that emerged in the aftermath of the Second World War. The intensification of this trend, which was all too evident during the financial crisis in 2008, has acquired an unprecedented momentum in the wake of the invasion of Ukraine.

One important symptom of the malaise afflicting the world order was the outbreak of the US-China trade war, which President Trump launched in 2018. Along with Britain's adoption of Brexit, it indicated that the trend toward economic nationalism had gained momentum. The absence of authoritative leadership by international organisations, such as the World Health Organisation, G20 or the EU during the Covid pandemic, served as an invitation to governments to further develop their national strategies. The subsequent conflict between states

108 https://www.spiked-online.com/2022/03/07/the-end-of-the-age-of-globalisation/

109 Zimmermann, K.F., Karabulut, G., Bilgin, M.H. and Doker, A.C. (2020) 'Inter-country distancing, globalisation and the coronavirus pandemic', *The World Economy*, vol. 43, no. 6, p. 1484.

110 Prashad, V. 'We Suffer from an Incurable Disease Called Hope', *TriContinental Newsletter* 48, November 6 2020, https://www.thetricontinental.org/newsletterissue/48-covid-vaccines

over pharmaceutical products exposed the irrelevance of these organisations in the face of a crisis. These developments called into question the capacity of international organisations to enforce their rules-based global order.

The rhetoric of free trade and international co-operation made sense to many influencers wedded to the belief that it was only a matter of time before globalisation would triumph over petty national squabbles. In contrast, today, policies associated with economic nationalism are regarded by many former globalists as a sensible response to the uncertainties prevailing in the international markets. During the pandemic, policymakers realised that they could not always rely on existing supply chains. Instead of outsourcing so much of their productive activities, they began to talk about building economic resilience through insourcing. Protectionism and autarky, which were once associated with the bad old days of the 1930s, gained new legitimacy on account of the pandemic-related shortages and disruptions.

The geopolitical shock of Russia's invasion of Ukraine has greatly amplified the disruptive effect of the economic shock of 2008 and the public health trauma of the Covid pandemic. Now that the maintenance of national security has become a challenge that no government can ignore, the world has entered a new geopolitical era. Global insecurity confronts all parts of the world, no matter how far from Ukraine. The former Australian prime minister Scott Morrison was in no doubt about the implication of this conflict for his country. He noted that 'the events unfolding in Europe are a reminder of the close relationship between energy security, economic security and national security'[111]. As events indicate, when national security is questioned, it is only a matter of time before policymakers opt for protectionist, national solutions to the economic problems they face. That is why the aftermath of Russia's invasion of Ukraine has seen the rise of autarky and the emergence of tension between economic blocs. Even within Europe, there is a growing competition for access to vital raw materials and energy sources[112].

Until recently, experts portrayed autarky and protectionist policies as so irrational that only a simple-minded populist could possibly advocate them. Populism was constantly attacked for investing its naïve faith in the nation-state. From their point of view, the nation-state could no longer shield people from the impact of the forces of globalisation. Articles and essays authored by globalist writers frequently highlighted trends that they associated with the 'end of the

---

111 https://www.reuters.com/article/australia-minerals-security-idCAKCN2LD09M
112 https://www.bloomberg.com/news/articles/2022-04-09/algeria-to-expand-natural-gas-exports-to-italy-by-almost-half

nation' or 'the demise of the nation state'[113]. Typically, they argued that nation-state had 'become obsolete' and the backlash to globalisation by populist movements was a symptom of their visceral reaction to the 'irreversible decline' of the nation. Anti-populist commentators took delight in emphasising the irrelevance of the nation and its supposed outdated institutions. In its place, the ideology of globalisation posited superior transnational institutions which would displace narrow-minded nationalist sentiments with their superior cosmopolitan values.

After the invasion of Ukraine, the much acclaimed omnipotent forces of globalisation are fast unravelling before our eyes. Numerous statements by economic commentators and geopolitical experts lament the 'End of Globalisation'. 'The End of Globalization?' is, in fact, the title of a recent contribution in *Foreign Affairs*[114]. In a similar vein, *The Economist* comments, 'Globalisation is dead and we need to invent a new world order'[115]. Larry Fink, the head of BlackRock, one of the world's largest investment corporations, warned that the 'Russian invasion of Ukraine has put an end to the globalisation we have experienced over the last three decades'[116]. At the May 2022 meeting of the World Economic Forum, it was obvious to those in attendance that globalisation had gone in reverse. On the eve of this meeting, Kristalina Georgieva, the head of the IMF, wrote in a blog that the world was confronted with a 'confluence of calamities' caused by the pandemic, high food and energy prices, tightening financial conditions to supply chains and the threat of climate change'[117]. Not even the most fervent advocate of the ideology of globalisation could ignore the return of geopolitics. Joachim Nagel, head of Germany's Central Bank, stated that the shift from globalisation was 'fuelled by geopolitical tensions and the desire to reduce economic dependencies'[118]. 'There is no silver bullet to address the most destructive forms of [global] fragmentation', noted Georgieva.

It is evident that Russia's invasion of Ukraine has called into question many of the geopolitical assumptions of the Western economic, political and cultural establishment. As in the past, when protectionism and autarky are ascendant, there is considerable potential for economic conflict to transform itself into an

---

113 https://www.theguardian.com/news/2018/apr/05/demise-of-the-nation-state-rana-das gupta

114 https://www.foreignaffairs.com/articles/world/2022-03-17/end-globalization

115 https://www.economist.com/open-future/2019/06/28/globalisation-is-dead-and-we-need-to-invent-a-new-world-order

116 https://www.ft.com/content/0c9e3b72-8d8d-4129-afb5-655571a01025

117 https://www.telegraph.co.uk/business/2022/05/22/economic-gloom-will-worsen-ukraine-war-causes-globalisation

118 https://www.ft.com/content/0c9e3b72-8d8d-4129-afb5-655571a01025

economic war. The speed with which Russia became the target of economic warfare indicates that we have arrived at the point where the line between politics and economics has become blurred. Consequently, the decoupling of economic blocs shows that the world economy is now subject to the logic of bitter inter-state rivalry.

However, it is important not to confuse the process of globalisation with its ideological expression. Globalisation, in the sense that it refers to the process of economic interaction among different people and nations in the world, has clearly not come to an end. Protectionism and economic nationalism notwithstanding, capitalism continues to transcend national borders, and the international division of labour remains relatively intact. But significantly, globalisation has lost its expansive dynamic. Moreover, the rules and expectations that governed global economic relations have lost much of their force. What's left is a form of globalisation that coexists with intense competition between conflicting national interests. Globalisation is now confronted with the growing challenge posed by economic nationalism.

Economic globalisation has gone into reverse. This coincides with the return of the nation-state and the apparent ineffectiveness of international institutions. Ukraine's heroic resistance has underlined the continuing relevance of national sovereignty. As Andrew Michta observed, 'after three decades of post-Cold War institutionalism and globalism, we are back to the fundamentals of national security: only a sovereign Ukraine can provide its citizens with a secure homeland'. He added that 'international institutions could not stop Putin from invading Ukraine[119]'. Yet again the experience of Ukraine highlights an important historical fact, which is that national security should not be outsourced to an external agency. It indicates that the willingness to take national sovereignty seriously is the *sine qua non* for defending the integrity of a nation.

Globalisation as an Ideology and a Political Project

Globalisation is often interpreted as the growing tendency of the world to become interconnected through trade, cultural exchange and the movement of people. However, globalisation is not simply a descriptive concept that touches on the internationalisation of social and economic life. It has also mutated into an ideology that elevates the status of international institutions and devalues the role of national governments. In effect, it promotes the idea that against

---

119 https://www.19fortyfive.com/2022/05/russias-invasion-of-ukraine-is-transforming-europe

the forces of the global market, national governments lack the power to determine the future of their countries. Consequently, this ideology renders politics pointless and condemns national sovereignty as an atavistic throwback to the bad old days of the 1930s. For globalist idealogues, patriotism and the celebration of a local community are regarded as an absurdity. In this vein, Carl Bildt, the former chair of the European Council on Foreign Relations, advanced the view that 'politics is gradually being reshaped into a contest between advocates of open, globalized societies and defenders of inward-looking tribalism'[120].

Bild's reference to tribalism connects with the classical imperialist rhetoric that assigned colonial subjects the status of inward-looking uneducated savages. If anyone personifies a zealous globalist ideologue, it is the Davos Man and former prime minister of Sweden, Carl Bildt. 'I must confess that I am a firm believer in the benefits of globalization', noted Bildt in his attack on national sovereignty[121]. For Bildt, globalism represents the very antithesis of economic nationalism. He naturally rejects the claim made by nation-oriented politicians that globalisation has not served the interests of a significant section of their societies.

Cosmopolitan ideologues have sought to represent globalisation as a medium for realising progressive objectives. From their standpoint, global institutions offered a positive alternative to the outdated and parochial practices of the nation-state. In recent decades, the standpoint of what its advocates describe as the 'cosmopolitan revolution' was most systematically articulated by Ulrich Beck.

Beck called for a 'cosmopolitan revolution' to overcome the 'lie of the national age', by which he meant the divisions and boundaries that allow the citizens of one nation to enjoy rights that are denied to others. He developed the concept of 'methodological cosmopolitanism' to refocus attention from what he perceived as the boundary-fixated consciousness of those who seek reassurance from the familiar lines drawn through the traditions of the nationally bounded imagination. Beck wrote that the 'basic concepts of "modern society"—*household, family, class, democracy, domination, state, economy, the public sphere, politics*, and so on' need 'to be released from the fixations of methodological nationalism and redefined and reconceptualized in the context of methodological cosmopolitanism'[122]. What Beck describes as the 'fixations of methodological na-

---

120 See https://www.weforum.org/agenda/2016/02/why-populism-is-on-the-rise-aecfc0ba-3f2b-4c03-8369-2f8247b74172

121 https://www.weforum.org/agenda/2017/02/carl-bildt-in-defence-of-globalization

122 Beck, U. (2005) *Power in the Global Age: A New Global Political Economy*, Polity Press: Cambridge p. 50.

tionalism' refers to the taken-for-granted meanings that influence and guide the behaviour of members of a community.

The project of de-legitimating so-called methodological nationalism has as its objective the authorisation of a borderless cosmopolitan society. In this way, the nation-state and a society linked to a nation are denuded of moral content and are subordinated to a borderless cosmopolitan order.

Cosmopolitanism even calls into question the status of national citizenship. It suggests that national citizenship has become irrelevant because the forces of globalisation have rendered boundaries porous and undermined the power of national institutions. Consequently, suggests one version of this argument, 'the future of citizenship must therefore be extracted from its location in the nation state'[123]. Another version proclaims that due to the supposed irrelevance of national borders and attachments, 'citizenship is becoming increasingly denationalized', and old forms of citizenship have been displaced by new ones, such as 'global citizenship', 'transnational citizenship' or 'postnational citizenship'[124]. The invention of the new metaphors for global citizenship is justified on the ground that citizenship is 'no longer unequivocally anchored in national political collectivities'[125].

According to supporters of methodological cosmopolitanism, just as borders have no moral significance, the people living within them have no legitimate distinct moral claims towards one another that do not apply to all humans. Beck takes the view that defining the duty and responsibility that members of a national community have towards one within a national border makes little sense. 'Why do we have to recognize a special moral responsibility towards other people just because, by accident, they have the same nationality?', he asks[126]. He also poses the rhetorical question of 'why should they be free of any moral sensibility towards other people for the sole reason that they happened to be born on the other side of the national fence?'. In other words, the ties that bind citizens together ought not impose any special duties that do not also apply to people living 'on the other side of the national fence'. From this perspective, the powerful sentiments that inspired the mobilisation of the people of Ukraine are difficult to understand.

123 Turner, B.S. (ed.) (1993) *Citizenship and Social Theory*, Sage: London, p. 14.

124 Bosniak, L. (1999) 'Citizenship denationalized', *Indiana Journal of Global Legal Studies*, vol. 7, no. 2, p. 449.

125 This is the view of the sociologist Yasemin Soysal, cited in Bosniak (1999), p. 454.

126 Beck, U. (2002) The cosmopolitan society and its enemies. *Theory, culture & society*, vol. 19. nos. 1–2, p.20.

The downgrading of the status of citizenship runs in parallel with a tendency to deny the relevance of democratic choice-making. From the cosmopolitan perspective, globalisation works as an omnipotent force that reduces the scope for sovereign decision-making. This outlook was clearly articulated by Alan Greenspan, the chairman of the U.S. Federal Reserve, when he stated in 2007: 'it hardly makes any difference who will be the next president. The world is governed by market forces'. And, as the historian Quinn Slobodian explained in his insightful study, *Globalists: The End of Empire And The Birth Of NeoLiberalism*, to the critics of Greenspan's world dominated by market forces, it looked like a new empire with 'globalization substituting for colonialism'[127].

With hindsight it is evident that globalisation was not merely about promoting the free flow of trade and capital. It was, above all, a political project, what Slobodian described as a project of 'politics and law'[128]. Despite their formal commitment to free markets, globalist neoliberals concluded that the world economy was far too important to be left to the discipline of economics or spontaneous forces of the market. Contrary to its free-market rhetoric, the project of globalism relied on international institutions regulating the world economy by enforcing their rules.

Phil Mullan has explained how the rule of international law created by the various global institutions reflected geopolitical realities. John Ikenberry, a globalist political scientist and apologist for the exercise of US hegemony, observed that Americans are less interested in ruling the world than in 'creating a world of rules'[129]. A similar point was echoed by the historian Adam Tooze, who argued that globalisation is 'an institution, an artefact of deliberate political and legal construction'[130].

In recent decades international institutions and organisations and NGOs have played an increasingly significant role in assuming decision making about matters that were historically the provenance of national governments. Many Western governments supported this trend to insulate themselves from domestic democratic pressure. The outsourcing of decision-making to organisations like the IMF, WTO or the EU allowed governments to avoid taking responsibility for the unpopular measures imposed on their citizens by these institutions. In effect, these globalist institutions sought to depoliticise decision-making, con-

---

127 Slobodian, Q. (2018) *Globalists: The End of Empire And The Birth Of NeoLiberalism*, Harvard University Press: Cambridge, Mass, p. 1.
128 Slobodian (2018), p. 92.
129 Cited in https://www.spiked-online.com/2019/03/15/globalism-a-world-in-chains
130 Tooze, A. (2018) *Crashed: How a Decade of Financial Crises Changed the World*, Allen Lane: London, p. 575.

strain the influence of national sovereignty and severely limit the workings of democracy. Back in 2015, Jean-Claude Juncker, the then-president of the European Commission, stated, 'There can be no democratic choice against the European treaties'[131]. In 2015, at the height of the eurozone debt crisis, when the majority of Greek voters rejected the EU-imposed bailout agreement, the German finance minister Wolfgang Schaeuble put matters bluntly, 'Elections change nothing. There are rules.'

Schäuble's indifference to the outcome of a democratically run election was justified on the ground that 'these are the rules'. His statement highlighted that the EU's rule of law serves as a political instrument and a medium of control that allows unelected judges to override the will of the people and the decisions made by legitimate national institutions. Yet it is precisely this type of governance that Fukuyama prescribed as the culmination of history. He wrote:

> 'I believe that the European Union more accurately reflects what the world will look like at the end of history than the contemporary United States. The EU's attempt to transcend sovereignty and traditional power politics by establishing a transnational rule of law is much more in line with a 'post-historical' world than the Americans' continuing belief in God, national sovereignty, and their military'[132].

Clearly Fukuyama's prediction, made in 1992, has not withstood the test of time. The globalist aspiration to transcend sovereignty can no longer ignore the reality in which geopolitical calculations challenge Fukuyama's 'post-historical' world. The vision of a post-historical world, a symptom of historical amnesia, has run up against a reality where history has the last word.

Today, Schäuble's claim that 'these are the rules' has lost much of its force. When competition gives way to conflict and potentially an economic war, the rules that have governed international relations since the Second World War settlement are no longer beyond question. Nor can the cosmopolitan downgrading of the nation-state's power be sustained in an era where it has acquired such formidable geopolitical significance. After the invasion of Ukraine, the claim that borders do not matter cannot be reconciled with reality.

131 https://www.bbc.co.uk/news/world-europe-31082656
132 Fukuyama, F. (2006) *The end of history and the last man*, Simon and Schuster: New York, p. 212.

The Rediscovery of Borders

The ideology of globalism is intensely hostile to national borders. It continually disparages national borders and the nation-state on the grounds of their supposed irrelevance to the contemporary world. Arguments supporting transnational, cosmopolitan ideals invariably claim that territorial borders – particularly those dividing nations – are artificial, accidental or arbitrary creations. Such borders are said to be in a constant state of flux, and groups of academic commentators now use the term 'bordering' to signify what some describe as a 'processual turn'[133]. The term bordering serves as a boundary-blurring concept that transforms fixed boundaries into constantly evolving and fluid ones.

Critics of national borders constantly draw attention to their historically contingent character. They frequently refer to national borders as an *invention* to underline their claim that there is nothing natural or normal about drawing territorial lines. Arguably, the feeble sensibility of historical consciousness in our time fosters a climate that regards the foundational political categories of Western societies as transient and arbitrary inventions. This tendency dominates academic literature on territorial borders. Commentators on this subject have adopted the patronising habit of informing their readers that borders dividing territories and especially nation-states did not always exist in the past. Such an argument today would deny the legitimacy of the defence of the border of Ukraine. Indeed, Russia uses the argument that these borders are a recent artificial invention to justify its invasion of Ukraine.

Another argument used to deny the moral status of borders and boundaries is a characterisation of such boundaries as accidental or arbitrary. Professor Martha Nussbaum's argument for a cosmopolitan, as opposed to a national focus for education, highlights the supposedly accidental origins of borders. She observed:

> 'An education that takes national boundaries as morally salient too often reinforces this kind of irrationality by lending what is an accident of history a false moral weight and glory'[134].

For Nussbaum, not only is the act of taking national borders seriously irrational, but it also smacks of 'false moral weight and glory'. The emphasis that cosmopolitan commentators attach to the accidental origins of borders is complement-

---

133 Yuval-Davis, Y, Wemyss, G. & Cassidy, K. (2019) *Bordering*, Polity Press: Cambridge, p. 18.
134 Nussbaum, M. (2002) 'Patriotism and Cosmopolitanism' in Nussbaum, M. (ed.) (2002) *For Love of Country*, Beacon Press: Boston, p. 11.

ed by a view of humans that ascribes an insignificant and random quality to their community affiliations. Indifferent to an individual's particularity and cultural connections, cosmopolitan campaigners dismiss these attributes as of little import. 'The accident of where one is born is just that, an accident; any human being might have been born in any nation', declared Nussbaum.[135] From the perspective of indifference to the place where one was born, the determination to sacrifice one's life to defend it makes little sense.

Advocates of borderlessness often drew inspiration from the apparent success of the European Union in eliminating border controls between most of its member states. Ulrich Beck has claimed that the 'defining characteristic of the European project was its "radical openness"'[136]. A similar argument was made by José Manuel Barroso, who declared that for Europe, openness is a 'congenital condition' that has been an 'integral part of our values since the beginning of the integration process'[137]. Beck stated that the 'cosmopolitan outlook' was founded on a 'global sense, a sense of boundarylessness'[138]. Though he recognised that the sense of boundarylessness created 'anguish' to those who lost their fixed reference points in life, he welcomed what he characterised as its 'reflexive awareness of ambivalences in a milieu of blurring differentiations and cultural contradictions'[139]. Certainly, the millions of Ukrainians fleeing their country are likely to wonder how they could regain their sense of fixed reference points.

The political expression of hostility towards borders is most consistently communicated by advocates of what might best be understood as the *New Federalism*.

Federalism is a mixed or compound mode of government that combines a general government with regional governments in a single political system, dividing the powers between the two. It has its roots in ancient Europe.

Federalism in the past was often linked to the project of nation-building – in Canada, the United States and Australia, the different units of these nations maintained jurisdiction over local affairs while co-existing within the jurisdiction of the national federal state.

---

135 Nussbaum (2002), p. 7.

136 Beck, U. (2003) 'Understanding the real Europe', *Dissent*, vol. 50, no. 3, p. 33.

137 See José Manuel Durão Barroso, President of the European Commission Europe's speech at the *International Forum* 2007: Barroso, J.M.D 'An open society in a globalised world', speech at the *International Forum*, "The economy and the open society", Milan, 8 May 2007, http://europa.eu/rapid/press-release_SPEECH-07-293_en.htm

138 Beck, U. (2006) *The Cosmopolitan Vision*, Polity Press: Cambridge p. 3.

139 Beck (2006) p. 3.

In contrast, the project promoted through New Federalism is not in the business of nation-building. On the contrary, it advocates transnational arrangements and wishes to deprive national entities of much of their sovereign power. The building of transnational federations requires the subordination of sovereignty – what it euphemistically characterises as *Shared Sovereignty*. New Federalism is a political project devoted to empowering international organisations with law-making authority that overrides the decision-making capacity of national institutions. It is motivated by the impulse to outsource decision-making to non-national international institutions whose role is underpinned by their technical competence or expertise – and most importantly, who are not accountable to any electorate and are therefore insulated from democratic pressure.

This principal goal of new federalists, to detach decision-making on important matters from the institutions of nation-states was epitomized by the Italian prime minister, Mario Draghi, when he urged the EU to respond to the war in Ukraine by deepening economic integration. Draghi went so far as to argue that the EU should abandon the requirement of unanimity on decisions to do with foreign policy and defence[140]. He stated that 'we must overcome this principle of unanimity', which 'leads to a logic of crossed vetoes, and move towards decisions taken by a qualified majority'. Draghi referred to his call for the EU to abandon its current requirement for most common foreign and security policy decisions to be adopted only by unanimity among member states as an instance of 'pragmatic federalism'.

The pursuit of 'pragmatic federalism' inexorably leads to the erosion of national sovereignty. If even defence and foreign affairs are outsourced to a transnational federal body, then little national sovereignty remains. That is precisely the point since the very idea of a nation is a historical relic for the New Federalists like Draghi.

The German cosmopolitan philosopher Jürgen Habermas adopted a tone of unadulterated contempt when he dismisses what he characterises as the 'caricature of national macrosubjects shutting themselves off from each other and blocking any cross-border democratic will-formation'. Predictably, such people are described as the adherents of 'right-wing populism'[141]. Beck regards national borders as the conveyors of the 'morality of exclusion'[142]. Like most New Feder-

---

140 https://www.ft.com/content/17276897-970f-4451-85bd-7a685cec0894
141 Habermas, J. (2016) *The Crisis of the European Union*, Polity Press: Cambridge, p. 48.
142 Beck (2002), p. 19.

alists, he assumes that just as borders have no moral significance, so the people living within them have no legitimate distinct moral claims towards one another that do not apply to all humans.

Commenting on the 'denigration of borders' by contemporary social theorists, the political scientist Sergei Prozorov has drawn attention to their alienation from and discomfort with boundaries[143]. Borders are understood as obstacles, represented as 'dividers of humanity and as expressions of particularisms'; they 'dominate, exclude, and exploit' and carry 'a legacy of congealed coercion and violence'[144]. Yet, as recent events confirm, the violation of borders represents the real threat to global peace.

The hostility of globalists towards borders and the nation coexists with a powerful sense of contempt for people who remain seriously attached to them. Such people are invariably labelled as narrow-minded, parochial xenophobes whose insecurity forces them to wrap themselves in their national flag. 'The populists, nationalists, stupid nationalists, they are in love with their own countries', declared a bemused Jean-Claude Juncker in May 2019 [145]. Juncker's incomprehension of how anyone could love their country was no doubt the genuine response of someone who regards spontaneous loyalties to community and to the borders surrounding it as an irritating feature of life. It is not surprising that Juncker was caught so unaware by the Russian invasion of Ukraine.

In contemporary cosmopolitan political discourse, nationalism and its cognate terms – national attachments, national identity, national sentiments – have acquired the kind of negative qualities that usually invite moral condemnation. In recent decades, even the nation-state's legitimacy has been put to question. This sentiment acquired a dominant influence amongst the Western intelligentsia in the post-Second World War era. As Johanna Möhring and Gwythian Prins pointed out, 'for more than two intellectual generations, since 1945, there has been an ascendant narrative in international affairs which has represented the nation state as pathological in its very nature'[146]. Such sentiments led many supporters of the EU to regard national sentiments as an expression of primitive attachments, which have absolutely no positive role to play in mod-

143 See Prozorov, S. (2008) 'De-limitation: the denigration of boundaries in the political thought of late modernity' in Parker, N. (ed.) (2008) *The Geopolitics of Europe's Identity: Centres, Boundaries and Margins*, Palgrave Macmillan: London.

144 O'Dowd, L. (2010) 'From a "Borderless World" to a "World of Borders"; bringing history back in', *Environment and Planning D: Society and Space*, vol. 28, no. 6, p. 1039.

145 See Sheftalovich, Z. 'Juncker lashes out at "stupid nationalist"', *Politico*, 23 May 2019. https://www.politico.eu/article/juncker-lashes-out-at-stupid-nationalists

146 Möhring, J. & Prins, G. (2013) *Sail On, O Ship Of State*, Notting Hill Editions: London, p. 1.

ern society. This view is most explicitly conveyed by academic cosmopolitan ide-alogues, who regard their crusade against nationalism as a sacred cause.

From the standpoint of New Federalism, organic ties to a nation's historical legacy, as well as community and family ties appear as obstacles to the emer-gence of an open, cosmopolitan, and transnational order. That is why the advo-cates of the New Federalism in the EU are not simply hostile to the principle and exercise of sovereignty but also to the cultural attachments associated with it. These include bonds of community, family, religion and culture. They tend to be hostile towards relatively homogenous national communities and prefer ones that lack the cohesion and solidarity of historically rooted cultures. Yet, in Ukraine, an effective resistance to Russian aggression was based on the kind of social bonds provided by a cohesive community that advocates of cosmo-politanism decry. It is not the people who perceive themselves as citizens of the world who are standing up against the Russian invaders. Instead, it is people who perceive themselves to be members of the Ukrainian nation who are at the forefront of the resistance.

Hostility towards borders adopts a peculiarly outraged tone when confronted with arguments that uphold the privileged political status of the citizen. The au-thority of citizenship, which has played a foundational role in the emergence of representative democracy, is now widely contested. The distinction between citi-zen and non-citizen is frequently condemned as unjust and exclusionary. Implic-itly, and in some cases explicitly, these arguments are directed at the normative foundation of a territorially based system of democracy.

The cosmopolitan de-nationalization of citizenship empties it of both mean-ing and content. The principle and exercise of citizenship are fundamental to the workings of a democratic society. Citizens possess important political rights and have responsibilities and duties towards other members of their community. Though the possession of citizenship through birth may seem arbitrary, it should nevertheless be seen as an inheritance that citizens share with others. That com-mon inheritance amongst members of a nation-state provides the foundation for solidarity between members of a community.

Citizenship is essentially a civic institution, and its legacy is inherited by ev-eryone born into it, including the children of families of former immigrants. Identification with the nation helps citizens – old and new – acquire a sense of intergenerational continuity, which provides a bond that offers a sense of per-manence and confidence. Historically, democrats of all shades of opinion recog-nised the importance of intergenerational continuity for the flourishing of civic society. Indeed, without the bonds supplied by intergenerational and other forms of community ties, it is difficult to imagine how Ukraine has managed to stand up to the onslaught of the Russian army.

As the political theorist Bernard Yack explains, 'the contingencies and vagaries of a shared memory and identity' are the foundations on which 'individual
rights and political freedoms are exercised'[147]. Indeed, it is those 'contingencies
and vagaries of a shared memory and identity' that motivates people in Ukraine
to demonstrate such remarkable acts of solidarity in the face of the Russian invaders. Without strong social bonds and identification with the nation, it is unlikely that the Government in Kyiv would have been able to mobilise so much
support, so swiftly for the defence of Ukraine.

Solidarity between people and the flourishing of a regime of social justice
requires that individuals understand the boundaries within which they engage
with one another. If we are to 'talk sense about social justice, we must know
what the relevant social and geographical boundaries are', notes the political
theorist Margaret Canovan[148], cautioning critics of national identity that:

> 'nations are not just common worlds; they are inherited common worlds, sustained by the
> facts of birth and the mythology of blood ... this natal element in political allegiance is cru-
> cially important, and is regularly forgotten by political theorists anxious to recommend a
> non-national version of political community[149].'

This view was shared by the political philosopher Hannah Arendt, who explained the inheritance of a common world binds people together in a manner
that allows them to identify with one another and their public institutions[150].
This forging of a relationship facilitates citizens to solidarise with one another
and take responsibility for the welfare and future of their society.

Criticism of national sovereignty and the status of citizenship is often made
through appealing to the superiority of universal and humanitarian values. However, universalism becomes a caricature of itself when it is transformed into a
metaphysical force that stands above the prevailing institutions through which
human beings make sense of the world. Humanity does not live above or beyond
the boundaries and institutions it created through great struggle and effort. At
least in one important respect, the New Federalists and Putin's regime share a
similar disposition, which is an indifference and cavalier attitude towards bor-

---

147 Quoted in: Kreuzer, P., and Weiberg, M. 'Framing Violence: Nation- and State-Building',
Peace Research Institute Frankfurt, 1 January 2005, www.jstor.org/stable/resrep14487

148 Canovan, M. (1996) *Nationhood and Political Theory*, Edward Elgar: Cheltenham, p. 28.

149 Canovan, M. (1999) 'Is there an Arendtian case for the nation-state?', *Contemporary Politics*, vol. 5, no. 2, p. 108.

150 Arendt, H. (1998) *The Human Condition*, 2nd ed., The University of Chicago Press: Chicago.

ders. A lack of respect for borders not infrequently goes hand-in-hand with empire building.

The Sovereignty of Bad Faith

The one crucial point that supporters of globalisation tend to underplay is that the heroes of Ukraine are defending the sovereignty of their nation. Given their hostility to the principle of national sovereignty, their support for its defence in Ukraine smacks of bad faith.

Many Western commentators wedded to a cosmopolitan outlook minimise the motivating force of national sovereignty and praise Ukrainians for fighting for cultural values similar to those of the Western political establishment. The US media, in particular, tends to represent Ukraine as on the 'right side of history' because it shares its system of values. President Zelensky and his colleagues are celebrated because they supposedly 'think like us'. This approach raises the question of whether they would support Ukraine's defence of national sovereignty if they did not 'think like us'.

Sometimes it appears that ethnocentric Westerners regard the issues at stake in the war in Ukraine as analogous to those fought out in their culture wars. Often, they represent Putin as a Russian version of Donald Trump. Writing in this vein in the *Guardian*, Thomas Zimmer warned that 'America's culture war is spilling into actual war-war'[151]. Almost effortlessly, Zimmer interweaved his hostility towards supporters of Donald Trump with his denunciation of Putin's Russia. Paul Krugman of the *New York Times* also could not resist the temptation of using Putin as a proxy for everything he hates about the kind of deplorables who backed Trump, Brexit and other supposedly populist causes and who go on 'whining about cancel culture'. He wrote:

> 'When I look at the United States, I worry that the West is, in fact, being made weaker by decadence—but not the kind that obsesses Putin and those who think like him. Our vulnerability comes not from the decline of traditional family values, but from the decline of traditional democratic values, such as a belief in the rule of law and a willingness to accept the results of elections that don't go your way[152].

---

151 https://www.theguardian.com/commentisfree/2022/mar/04/americas-culture-war-is-spilling-into-actual-war-war
152 https://www.nytimes.com/2022/03/28/opinion/putin-western-decadence.html

Taking a pop at Trump and people who worry about gender neutrality and the state of the American family, Krugman also has a go at those who still have respect for masculine norms. He warned, 'Modern wars aren't won with swaggering machismo'.

In a *New York Times* opinion piece titled 'Putin's Proxy Culture War', Michelle Goldberg sought to rally her readers to her side of this conflict. As far as she is concerned, 'Ukraine has been waging a globalized culture war of its own, trying to rally the world to an idealized liberal internationalism'[153]. Goldberg wished to recruit the people of Ukraine and its President Zelensky to her liberal internationalist worldview. She wrote that Zelensky 'speaks to the highest aspirations of Western audiences who've been starved for inspiration'. Taking a more objective stance, her colleague David Brooks notes 'Globalization Is Over. The Global Culture Wars Have Begun'[154]. He reported that 'Globalization has been replaced by something that looks a lot like global culture war' and explains:

'Economic rivalries have now merged with political, moral and other rivalries into one global contest for dominance. Globalization has been replaced by something that looks a lot like global culture war.'

Brooks, like his co-thinkers, could not help but regard Ukraine as a moral resource for strengthening the legitimacy of the values upheld by advocates of globalisation. He concludes by assuring his readers that 'what we call "the West" is not an ethnic designation or an elitist country club' for 'the heroes of Ukraine are showing that at its best, it is a moral accomplishment, and unlike its rivals, it aspires to extend dignity, human rights and self-determination to all'. It appears that the 'heroes of Ukraine' serve as an advertisement for the American way of life.

The principal form assumed by the sovereignty of bad faith is to represent the Ukrainian aspiration for self-determination as a type of nationalism that is not really nationalist. 'Under Russian bombardment, Ukrainians are redefining nationalism' is the report title in the *New Statesman*. It reassures readers that 'many Ukrainians have made a conscious effort to embrace their multi-ethnic present'. The author, Emily Tamkin, asserts that the threat posed by Putin has ushered 'into being a new, civic, multi-ethnic Ukrainian nationalism'[155]. In recent years there has been a conscious project of framing Ukrainian nationalism as an

---

153 https://www.nytimes.com/2022/03/28/opinion/putin-culture-war.html
154 https://www.nytimes.com/2022/04/08/opinion/globalization-global-culture-war.html
155 https://www.newstatesman.com/world/europe/ukraine/2022/03/under-russian-bombard ment-ukrainians-are-redefining-nationalism

outlook that shares the values of cosmopolitan idealogues. In this way, Ukrainian nationalism is relieved of the burden of guilt that cosmopolitan globalists usually attach to nationalism.

Many Western supporters of Ukraine stop short of offering genuine and unconditional backing for the right of this nation to exercise its sovereignty. There are frequent calls by the West to 'accept reality in Ukraine'[156]. Before the outbreak of the war, there were numerous calls on Western leaders to encourage Ukrainians to compromise and learn to accept a form of quasi-independence. 'Preventing a war is the best thing that the US and its allies can do to preserve Ukraine's well-being, if not the ideal of full independence', wrote Nancy Qian in *Project Syndicate*, a couple of weeks before the outbreak of the war. At a different time, Mario Draghi, the Italian prime minister, Olaf Scholz, the chancellor of Germany, and Emmanuel Macron, the president of France, suggested Ukraine should be ready to cede some of her territory in exchange for peace with Russia.

Western commentators frequently advised Ukraine to embrace neutrality and accommodate Russia's foreign policy interests and security concerns during the past two decades. Even when such advice is made with the best intentions, it is not up to foreign players to dictate how Ukraine should exercise its sovereignty.

The war is fundamentally a conflict over whether or not Ukraine can be a fully independent and sovereign nation. There are many issues at stake in this war; the most fundamental of which is disagreement over Ukraine's borders. To those wedded to a borderless outlook, fighting a war seems like a pointless throwback to the bad old days of the 19th and 20th centuries. However, with the unravelling of the global order, borders between nations are likely to become more contentious. That is why it is so important for the West to wake up from its long hibernation and relearn the importance of taking borders and the value of sovereignty seriously.

156 https://www.project-syndicate.org/commentary/ukraine-russia-has-stronger-interest-than-west-by-nancy-qian-1-2022-02

Chapter 4
Presentism and the Loss of the Sense of the Past

Diplomacy is an art that has been not so much lost as shredded in recent decades. For centuries Western Governments prided themselves on the sophistication of their diplomatic relations, the depth of their international historical knowledge and their confidence in semi-confidential exchanges and "back-channels". It informed decision making at the highest levels. Not so, now.

Writing of a series of blunders committed by successive British Governments in recent decades, the historian Anthony Seldon highlighted the inability of politicians to avoid the errors of the past[157]. He criticised institutional practices that have led to a narrow presentist mode of operation:

> 'The rapid churn of ministers and senior officials, decline in use of documents, the rise of tribal special advisers and ideological think tanks militate against drawing on history. New ministers and their teams arrive bursting with contempt for their predecessors. Institutional memory is junked unceremoniously. The old guard are booted out to make way for zealots high on histrionics and low on history'.

Seldon quite rightly criticises the absence of a sense of history that leaves policymaking adrift. He concluded that 'embedding at least history-informed, and ideally history-rich, policymaking at our heart is no longer a luxury but a necessity'. The loss of institutional memory and a culture of historical illiteracy is widespread within the offices of the state in the Anglo-American world.

Every new cohort of consultants, experts or political advisors that enters an office of the states take pleasure in denouncing the 'old way of doing things' and demanding that past practices be scrapped. Government bureaucracies have become captivated with the latest management techniques, which are devoted to celebrating what is new and modern. Calls for a 'Management Mindset' in the US Department of State are invariably followed by a demand for techniques of performance management and the introduction of the latest fads circulating in the world of business[158]. According to a contribution published by the Washington based Institute for the Study of Diplomacy, 'the diplomatic service needs to employ modern management techniques, beginning by flattening the hierarchy

---

157 https://www.thetimes.co.uk/article/historians-can-help-politicians-avoid-errors-of-the-past-n38n9p0h9
158 See for example https://afsa.org/needed-management-mindset

https://doi.org/10.1515/9783110981544-006

and empowering employees to fulfil their mandates, and it needs to promote a cultural shift where innovation, risk taking, outstanding performance are rewarded'[159].

In the realm of geopolitics, change management techniques encourage a new form of diplomacy that is more harmonious with the practices of private organisations or large non-governmental organisations than with an institution of a state devoted to the pursuit of national interest. As one advocate of the new 'knowledge diplomacy' explained:

> 'Contemporary diplomacy is changing at an unprecedented pace and is characterised by new actors, new issues and new functions. The shift from a state-based approach, typically centred on the role of ministries of foreign affairs and professional diplomats, to a multi-actor approach is a hallmark of the current changes'[160].

The downgrading of the status of the professional diplomat along with a shift away from a 'state-based approach' has important implications for the conduct of foreign affairs. Calculations regarding geopolitical matters compete with an outlook wedded to a managerial ethos. This approach is usually justified on the ground that unprecedented change demands new flexible forms of organisation. The rhetoric of 'unprecedented change' serves to legitimate what is fast becoming a dogma of novelty. Unfortunately, calls to adopt new management performance models inevitably lead to a loss of institutional continuity. It also leads to a loss of institutional memory. In a small organisation dealing with collecting local taxes, the loss of institutional memory need not have major implications for other parts of the country or of the world. However, the loss of memory by government departments dealing with foreign affairs can have profound and disruptive global consequences. To make matters worse, within these departments, the proportion of professional diplomats has decreased while the number of technocratically minded bureaucrats has increased.

The turn of institutions dealing with diplomacy towards performance management coincides with the politicisation of foreign affairs departments. This trend, which is widespread within the institutions of Western states, is most evident in the United States. According to the Association For Diplomatic Studies and Training, between 1975 to 2013, the proportion of Foreign Service Officers in senior positions, 'has declined from over 60 per cent to between 25–30 per

159 https://medium.com/the-diplomatic-pouch/analysis-a-third-of-u-s-diplomats-are-eyeing-the-exits-that-might-be-a-good-thing-8470e6fb2989
160 https://www.universityworldnews.com/post.php?story=20180214084632675

cent'[161]. The report indicates that this shift has led to a 'loss of long-term field perspective'. Knowledge essential for the conduct of diplomacy requires a sophisticated grasp of foreign languages and cultures and an understanding of history. It also requires an ethos of professionalism and service. Today, the quality of many individuals making vital judgment calls on matters about foreign affairs is conspicuously not up to the task. They often lack the depth of knowledge and sophistication required for dealing with issues such as the ones that surrounded the decades long tension between Russia and Ukraine. The tragic consequences of geopolitical illiteracy amongst officials and supposedly professional diplomats was fully exposed during debacle in Afghanistan in 2021.

The loss of its authoritative status by the British Foreign Office has been widely commented on. This department, once regarded as the 'Rolls-Royce of Whitehall', has lost much of its prestige. Professor Michael Clarke, former director of the Royal United Services Institute, noted that this organisation 'is at the lowest level of operational competence and respect than at any time in the 45 years I have been studying UK external policy[162]. When the British Foreign Secretary Liz Truss confused the Baltic and the Black Sea when pledging to support Ukraine, she let the world know that her department no longer possessed an eye for detail[163]. Similar blunders by President Biden – such as confusing Hungarians with Ukrainians – are not simply an expression of personal defects[164]. They are symptomatic of a cavalier and unprofessional approach that underestimates the issues at stake. This trend is also evident in France, where members of the diplomatic service threatened to go on strike because of the introduction of so-called reforms that would lead to its de-professionalisation[165].

Many influences have contributed to the diminishing effectiveness of Western diplomacy. But the loss of historical memory coupled with the institutionalisation of historical amnesia has seriously eroded its geopolitical intelligence. The prevailing technocratic obsession with novelty – strikingly illustrated by the ascendancy of 'change management' – is characteristically coupled with the tendency to disparage values and practices associated with the past. Within

161 https://adst.org/american-diplomacy-at-risk/

162 https://www.ft.com/content/422629e4-5219-4dfa-a2ab-e06a0410f50f

163 https://www.dailymail.co.uk/video/vladimirputin/video-2604297/Video-Liz-Truss-confuses-Baltic-Black-Sea-700-miles-apart.html

164 https://hungarytoday.hu/joe-biden-confuse-hungarians-ukrainians-ukraine-war-javenils-us/

165 https://www.thetimes.co.uk/article/emmanuel-macron-at-war-as-french-foreign-service-staff-walkout-over-reforms-pp6vrzszt

official circles and especially in the world of business administration, the phenomenon of historical amnesia encourages the tendency to cancel the past.

The prevailing regime of historical amnesia has encouraged Western Elites to forget both the origins of the predicament they face and the relationship between the present and the past. This sensibility influences the way they interpret geopolitical and military issues. Many of them operated on the assumption that in an era of globalisation, conflicts between nation-states had lost much of their significance. At some point, sections of the elites began to believe that their globalised world was freed from the burden of the past. They claimed that conventional wars were fast becoming an endangered species. Accordingly, the role and authority of the military were downsized. So-called security experts claimed that the main threat they faced was Islamic or cyber terrorism and other non-state actors.

Many diplomats and so-called experts attached to the American State Department or the British Foreign Office suffer from historical amnesia and therefore find it difficult to grasp their country's geopolitical interests. Many of them lack language skills and imagine that in a post-national world, different leaders can understand one another because they share similar cosmopolitan values. That is why for some time, what appeared to excise Western leaders about Putin was not his geopolitical ambitions but his failure to sign up to their cultural values on gender and sexuality.

Former US President Barack Obama personified the geopolitical illiteracy dominating western diplomacy. He interpreted his relation to Russia through the prism of America's culture war. His approach was spelt out in his address to the Youth of Europe Conference in March 2014[166]. In that speech, he linked his criticism of Russia's occupation of Crimea with his opposition to certain, apparently 'backward' cultural values back home in the US. He celebrated the politics of identity and permissiveness and denounced what he characterised as the 'older, more traditional view of power'. He said that 'instead of targeting our gay and lesbian brothers and sisters' – as Russia does – 'we can use our laws to protect their rights'. Effortlessly Obama jumped from Russia's seizure of Crimea to a celebration of identity politics and American attitudes towards the politics of sex. A loss of clarity about geopolitical matters ensues when diplomacy is intertwined with identity politics.

---

166 https://obamawhitehouse.archives.gov/the-press-office/2014/03/26/remarks-president-address-european-youth

Presentism

The loss of the sense of the past has had a corrosive impact on the conduct of international affairs. This sensibility is underwritten by the assumption that we live in a world of accelerated change – one that simply renders the past irrelevant. The term New Normal is frequently used in obituaries about the past. The author of *Organizing for the New Normal* claims that 'in today's world, everything seems to be happening much more quickly'[167]. He argues that since the world is changing 'exponentially,' companies must be ready to embrace the new constantly. 'There is no time to rest, no time to admire their efforts, no time to think', he concludes. When the mantra of 'there is no time to think' turns into a dogma, those in charge of foreign affairs are always playing catch up.

Scholars have characterised the perception of rapid change and its widespread institutionalisation as the 'acceleration of history'. The term, acceleration of history was first advanced by the French historian Daniel Halévy, who concluded that the dominant and permanent feature of modern society has ceased to be permanence and continuity but change. Drawing on Halévy's work, the French historian François Hartog elaborated the concept of "presentism". According to Hartog, presentism is 'the sense that only the present exists, a present characterized at once by the tyranny of the instant and by the treadmill of an unending now'[168]. The cultural imperative of presentism exercises a profound influence on the attitude of western society towards the past. In particular, presentism encourages a shift in the site of legitimation from the past to the future. It encourages an attitude of disdain towards historical precedents and the legacy of the past.

Presentism not only cuts off the present from the past, it also collapses the distinction between the present and the future. If indeed change is so rapid that nothing can be taught and all that can be done is to learn to react, then the future becomes our permanent present. In all but name history comes to an end. This sense of terminus – that invariably characterises presentism – has as its symptom confusions about temporality. The German sociologist Hartmut Rosa invented the concept of *frenetic standstill*. Frenetic standstill refers to a social condition where 'the sense that, while everything seems to change faster and faster, real or structural social change is no longer possible'.[169] Back in the

---

167 Markides, C. (2021) *Organizing for the New Normal*, Kogan Page: London.

168 Hartog F. (2017) *Regimes of Historicity: Presentism And experiences of Time*, Columbia University Press: New York, p. xv.

169 Rosa, H. (2013) 'Conclusion: Frenetic Standstill? The End of History', *Social Acceleration*, Columbia University Press: New York.

19th century, the German philosopher Friedrich Nietzsche voiced this sentiment when he wrote that European culture was 'moving towards a catastrophe, with a tortured tension that is growing from decade to decade, relentlessly, violently, like a river that wants to reach the end'[170].

Presentism is underpinned by a theory of rapid change – acceleration of time – that cuts off the present from the past and collapses the distinction between the present and the future so that the problem projected to the future becomes our own. So instead of us influencing the future, the future shapes our lives today. In a sense, the present has extended into 'both the future and the past'[171]. Presentism works as an unending now.

The idea that due to the acceleration of history, the present has become detached from the past was first raised in the 19th century. The French writer and historian François-René Chateaubriand wrote in the preface to his *Essay* in 1826 that 'events moved faster than my pen'. In 1831 he noted that he was writing ancient history, while modern history was knocking on his door; and it 'thundered past'[172]. In the United States, Henry Adams elaborated the theory of the Law of Acceleration. According to Adams, events move so fast that 'every past example is always too late'. In his study, published in 1919, Adams concluded that the rapid pace of change meant there was little point in teaching the young about the past facts. He stated that 'all the teacher could hope for was to teach (the mind) reaction'[173].

The loss of the sense of the past was not simply an outcome of society's perception of hyper-change. The sensibility of an ever-widening psychic distance between the present and the past was shaped by dramatic historical experiences – the most important of which was the First World War.[174] Members of the European cultural and political elites concluded that this catastrophic war had created an insurmountable rupture between the present and the past.

Disconnected from the past, Western societies found it difficult to develop a compelling narrative to socialise its young. At this point, the phenomenon known today as the 'generation gap' acquired a powerful cultural significance. The cultural gap that opened up between the post-First World War world and the pre-war era would, in the decades to follow, gradually lead Western society to turn its back on its past. At some point in the 20th century, the Western world

---

170 Nietzsche, F. (1967) *The Will To Power*, Random House: New York, p. 3.
171 Hartog (2017), p. 201.
172 Cited in Hartog (2017), p. 80.
173 Adams, H. (2019) *The Education of Henry Adams*, Good Press: New York.
174 See Furedi, F. (2014) *First World War – Still No End In Sight*, Bloomsbury: London, chapters 1 & 2.

became estranged from the authoritative status of the past and often adopted the attitude of rejecting it altogether. Its obituary was captured by the title of the historian J.H. Plumb's book, *The Death Of The Past* (1969).[175] Though Plumb was sympathetic to the loss of authority of the past; he was sensitive to the fact that something important was lost. He observed that 'whenever we look, in all areas of social and personal life, the hold of the past is weakening'[176].

In the 1930s, the German philosopher Edmund Husserl wrote about how Western society was caught up in the 'spell' of 'our times'. He feared that the powerful mood of presentism, which has overtaken society, led to a 'cultural breakdown, weariness of spirit and disintegration'[177]. Being caught up in the spell of the present acquired an unprecedented influence since the end of the Cold War. Since that time, the conviction that rapid change renders the past irrelevant has acquired the status of dogma amongst policymakers. Presentism has exercised a powerful influence on educational and social theory. David Inglis's comment on 'the death of history in British sociology' speaks to the cultural condition of historical amnesia that prevails in the social science university departments of the West.[178]

The sense of terminus that accompanies presentism gained hold in the1970s when the future oriented ideologies of modernity became exhausted. Utopian visions and even idealistic views about the possibility of positive social transformation gradually gave way to more downbeat even dystopian view of the future. Estranged from the past and now alienated from future, Western societies unconsciously adopted presentism as a way of life.

Presentism detaches itself from the past to the point that it continually perceives what preceded it – its conventions and ideals – as having come to an end. This sentiment frequently attaches itself to long-established historical trends. Even important, relatively recent events are confined to a folder in the archives marked the Past. That is why so many commentators concluded that Russia's invasion of Ukraine in 2014 did not necessarily serve as a precedent for conflicts in the future. So on 16 February, 2022 – a week before Russia's invasion of Ukraine – the headline of an essay published by the American think-tank, Atlantic Coun-

---

175 Plumb, J.H. (1986) *The Death of the Past*, Macmillan: London.

176 Plumb, J.H. (1969), p. 66.

177 See Moran, D. (2012) *Husserl's Crisis of the European Sciences and Transcendental Phenomenology: An Introduction*, CUP: Cambridge, pp. 11 & 26.

178 Inglis, D. (2010b) 'The death of history in British sociology: Presentism, intellectual entrepreneurship and the conundra of historical consciousness' in Burnett, J., Jeffers, S., and Thomas, G. (eds.) (2010) *New Social Connections: Sociology's Subjects and Objects*, Palgrave: Basingstoke.

cil could confidently assert that 'Putin Won't Invade Russia'[179] Three days before the invasion *BBC News* offered its readers a commentary titled 'Ukraine Crisis: Five Reason Why Putin Might Not Invade'[180].

The outlook of presentism has desensitised many Western diplomats and experts from the coming to terms with some of the unresolved historical questions and concerns facing the people of the former Soviet Bloc. The painful memories of a dark 20th century continue to haunt millions of people on both sides of the war being fought out on the battlefields of Ukraine. When I talk to Hungarian people living near the border of Ukraine it becomes evident that they perceive the conflicts of past as recent events. So do millions of Poles, who fear that after Ukraine they could be next. As far as they are concerned, history has not ended and they cannot even take their sovereignty as a nation for granted. There is no conflict-free end in sight in this part of the world.

The counterpoint to the declaration that this is the *end* is the proliferation of the prefix 'post' to various phenomena. To terms such as post-industrial, post-scarcity or post-modern were added post-historical, post-nationalism, post-national, and post-border. These terms aim to decouple the present from the past. As Brook Thomas wrote, the 'post' implies a 'belatedness, an age in which everything has always already occurred'[181].

Endism speaks to an ahistorical imagination that overlooks how the legacy of the past imposes its influence over contemporary life. This outlook is underwritten by a powerful impulse to detach the present from the past. Even a sensitive historian like John Lukács has embraced this endist sensibility when he declared that 'It's the End of the Modern Age' and claimed that we are witnessing, 'not *fin de siecle*, but *'fin d'une ere'*[182]. This is a sensibility that is deeply embedded in the current zeitgeist. 'I sense a period ending,' observed the historian of the post-Cold War, Mary Elise Sarotte, in her commentary on Russia's invasion of Ukraine.[183] In contrast, if one breaks out of the presentist mould and takes a longer historical view, it is possible to see important continuities with the past.

Almost unannounced, the kind of war that many Europeans believed would no longer blight their continent has suddenly erupted with a vengeance. Some

179 https://www.atlanticcouncil.org/blogs/new-atlanticist/why-putin-wont-invade-ukraine/
180 https://www.bbc.co.uk/news/world-europe-60468264
181 Thomas, B. (1991), *The new historicism: and other old-fashioned topics*, Princeton University Press: Princeton, NJ, p. 200.
182 Lukacs, J., 'It's the End of the Modern Age', *The Chronicle of Higher Education*, 26 April 2002, http://chronicle.com/free/v48/i33/33b00701.htm
183 https://www.nytimes.com/2022/03/01/opinion/russia-ukraine-cold-war.html

interpret this war as heralding the end of the 'Old World Order'[184]. This interpretation reflects an illusion about the stability of the globalist post-Cold War era. The war in Ukraine indicates that despite the Western commentariat's best efforts, we are not done with the past. The very difficult questions raised and re-raised during a succession of violent conflicts are still in search of a satisfactory answer

Making Sense of Year Zero History

Endism is general, and the claim that history has come to an end, in particular, finds its clearest expression in what can be described as Year Zero History. As we noted previously, the emergence of Year Zero History is fuelled by the impulse of disrupting historical continuity. This trend is partly fuelled by the palpable sense of estrangement of Western society from its historical legacy. The alienation of Western culture transcends the conventional ideological divide. Such sentiments are not confined to the radical post-modernists. Even mainstream liberal and conservative thought in the West has become emotionally disconnected from the past.

The call to detach the present from the past is widely embraced by cosmopolitan thinkers and policymakers who are bitterly hostile to national histories, emphasising a narrative of continuity with the nation's past. In recent decades the most vociferous opponents of narratives that draw on a nation's continuity with the past are German commentators, who wish to distance themselves from their nation's Nazism (repetition of past). Their arguments seize upon the horrors of the Holocaust to conclude that national histories that draw on historical continuity constitute a danger to society. In this way, the project of detaching the present from the past serves the cosmopolitan goal of displacing national with a post-national outlook.

In its most dramatic form, post-nationalist thinkers call for the disavowal of the past and for a thoroughgoing break with everything that occurred before 1945. This rejection does not mean that they are not interested in the politics of memory. On the contrary, they talk constantly about the gory details of history – such as slavery and the Holocaust – to instrumentally deploy them as cautionary tales against their ideological foes. The refrain 'it is just like the 1930s' serves

184 See   https://www.theatlantic.com/international/archive/2022/02/us-europe-russia-putin-new-world/622917/

as a front-line rhetorical weapon to discipline those who defy transnational conventions.

Their main target is the affirmation of historical continuity, which is often justified on the grounds that after the Holocaust, appeals to the legacy of the past and historical continuity must be cast aside. This proposition is most forcefully asserted by the prominent German philosopher Jürgen Habermas for whom a total break from 'historical life' is an ethical imperative. He warned that;

> 'Auschwitz has become the signature of an entire epoch – and this concerns all of us. Something happened there that no one could previously have thought possible. It touched a deep layer of solidarity among all who wear a human face. Until then – despite the monstrosities of world history – we had simply taken the integrity of this deep layer for granted. A band of naivete was torn to shreds at Auschwitz – a naivete from which unquestioning traditions had drawn their authority, from which historical continuities in general had lived. Auschwitz altered the conditions for the continuation of historical life – and not only in Germany'[185].

At first sight, the anti-historical thesis proposed by Habermas appears as a thoughtful attempt to draw attention to the singular significance of the Holocaust. But on closer inspection, his endeavour to turn the Holocaust into a secular version of original sin turns this tragedy into a moralistic exhortation for constituting a new form of personhood. Habermas's narrative of the Fall of Men demands that people renounce their past and their traditions, nationality, and history. The principal target of this narrative is the consciousness of historical continuity.

Since the 1980s, even the slightest interest in national history was treated with suspicion, and in some circles, 'national history' was condemned as an accomplice to xenophobic politics. 'We, historians, need to reflect on how to deal with national histories especially after they have demonstrated to be so dangerous in the past by legitimating wars and genocides,' argued one of its opponents[186]. Historians like Stefan Berger portray national histories as a dangerous virus that needs to be quarantined. He has argued that such a containment strategy demands that the 'naturalisation' and 'essentialisation' of national narratives should be forcefully 'denaturalised and 'de-essentialised' to reduce the harms they can cause. He also asserted that the threat posed by national history

185 Habermas, J. (1989) 'Historical consciousness and post-traditional identity: remarks on the Federal Republic's Orientation to the West', *Acta Sociologica*, vol. 31, no. 1.
186 Martín-Arroyo, P. (2015) *"Histoeuropeanisation": Challenges and Implications of (Re)writing the History of Europe "Europeanly", 1989–2015*, College of Europe Natolin Campus: Warszawa, p. 45.

should be limited by the creation of 'kaleidoscopic national histories' that recast national memory into multiple diverse fragments[187].

Opponents of historical continuity often display an obsessive anachronistic orientation towards the past. Events – historical and literary- are evaluated from the standpoint and values of today. According to this imperative of cultural anachronism, centuries-old historical figures and literary characters from the past are castigated for their racism or sexism or classism or whatever offends the imagination of the contemporary author. Paradoxically, presentism encourages an attitude of anachronism, whereby cultural commentators and political idealogues casually cross the line between the present and the past.

The tendency to read history backwards as if it were merely a reflection of the present has acquired a variety of forms. In recent times one of the most widely practised examples of presentism is the claim that 'it is just like the thirties'. Taken out of its historical context, the thirties have become the analogy of choice used by all sides in political debates and conflicts over cultural values. In recent political controversies throughout the West, the behaviour of adversaries is constantly represented as if they are the 21st version of 20th century Nazism.

Since Russia's invasion of Ukraine, all sides appear to be obsessed with accusing the other side of behaving 'just like the Nazis'. At times, Vladimir Putin presents himself as a latter-day Stalin, fighting the Great Patriotic War of the 1940s. When Putin launched his invasion, he justified his 'special operation' on the ground that it aimed to 'demilitarise and de-nazify Ukraine'. He frequently repeated this claim, and during his Victory Day speech in Moscow in May 2022, he told Russian soldiers that they are 'fighting for the same thing their fathers and grandfathers did' – for 'the Motherland'[188]. In turn, the Western media and politicians also play the Nazi card and constantly resort to the refrain that 'Putin is behaving just like the fascists' For example, the British Secretary of Defence declared that Putin was 'mirroring' the fascism of Nazi Germany. He stated that 'through the invasion of Ukraine, Putin, his inner circle and generals are now mirroring the fascism and tyranny of 70 years ago'[189].

The anachronistic thinking of the current era leads newspaper commentators to ask, 'Is Vladimir Putin the new Adolf Hitler? Is Russia a fascist danger

187 Berger, S. (2007) 'Writing National Histories in Europe: Reflections on the Pasts, Presents and Futures of a tradition' in Jarusch, K.H., and Lindenberger, T. (eds.) (2007) *Conflicted memories: Europeanizing Contemporary Histories*, Berghahn Books: Oxford, pp. 65–66.

188 See Tim Black's essay on Putin's plundering of history in https://www.spiked-online.com/2022/05/09/putins-shameful-abuse-of-history/

189 https://www.telegraph.co.uk/world-news/2022/05/08/vladimir-putin-mirroring-nazis-says-ben-wallace/

to world peace, as was Nazi Germany?' before answering, 'the parallels are disturbingly familiar'[190]. One political scientist, Alexander Motyl, declared, 'Yes, Putin and Russia are fascist'[191]. And Mateusz Morawiecki, the Polish prime minister, stated that Putin's 'monstrous ideology' poses a 'deadly threat to Europe'. He claimed that Putin was more dangerous than Adolf Hitler or Joseph Stalin[192].

It is particularly worrying when professional historians make tenuous and strained comparisons between Putin's Russia and Nazi Germany. Thus Timothy Snyder, a professor of history at Yale University, declared, 'We should say it. Russia is Fascist'. To validate his argument, he adopted the thesis that claims that fascism is defined principally by 'the triumph of will over reason'[193]. If one was to rely on this ahistorical definition, literally every unreasonable pursuit of violence – from the pursuit of violence by the Spanish Inquisition in the 15th century to jihadist aggression in 20th century Syria – could be described as fascistic. Pointing to the violent atrocities committed by Russia in Ukraine, Snyder noted;

'A time traveller from the 1930s would have no difficulty identifying the Putin regime as fascist. The symbol Z, the rallies, the propaganda, the war as a cleansing act of violence and the death pits around Ukrainian towns make it all very plain'.

As it happens, a time traveller with even a modest sense of historical consciousness would know that contemporary Russia bears no relationship to the fascist states of the 1930s. Such a time traveller would know that the appalling behaviour of Russian troops notwithstanding, comparing their actions with those of the fascists trivialises the unique tragedy of World War Two and the Holocaust.

The attempt to promote the view that 'it is just like the thirties' is often motivated by the best of intentions. Still, such a simplistic interpretation of the behaviour of Russia fails to capture the issues at stake in this war. It also shows a misunderstanding of the unique and distinct dynamic and features of the rise of fascism in the 1930s. For example, Italy, Spain and Germany in the 1930s served as a terrain for intensely bitter rivalries between competing ideologies. In the first instance, fascism constituted a response to a domestic threat from political forces that were perceived as constituting a deadly threat to the nation's integrity.

190 https://eu.beaconjournal.com/story/opinion/columns/2022/05/09/retired-kent-state-professor-says-war-in-ukraine-shows-how-vladimir-putin-is-like-hitler/9643814002/
191 https://theconversation.com/yes-putin-and-russia-are-fascist-a-political-scientist-shows-how-they-meet-the-textbook-definition-179063
192 https://www.telegraph.co.uk/world-news/2022/05/10/vladimir-putin-dangerous-adolf-hitler-joseph-stalin/
193 https://www.nytimes.com/2022/05/19/opinion/russia-fascism-ukraine-putin.html

Mussolini's March on Rome in October 1922 was preceded by what was widely perceived as a threat from the growing power of the Italian Communist Party. Domestic political conflict on anything like the scale experienced in the 1930s has been conspicuously absent in Russia for a very, very long time.

A Disneyfied version of the 1930s does little to illuminate the current situation in Ukraine. Understanding the relationship between history and geopolitics is essential for making sense of the current era, but a sense of historical specificity is required. If the authors of the 'just like the thirties' really took their arguments seriously, they would have no choice but to demand that their government get ready for an imminent global war.

Understandably the pathologisation of the past and Year Zero history was and remains particularly powerful in Germany, where memories of the catastrophic Nazi experience haunted many members of the post-World War Two younger generations. Calls for an absolute break with Third Reich and the past were expressed in the concepts of *Stunde Null* or *Nullpunkt*, Zero Hour or Zero Point. In 1945, there were many 'declarations by members of a younger generation decrying the bankruptcy of the older generation and indeed of the entire German cultural tradition'[194]. Though principally confined to Germany, the cause of making a radical break with the past gained adherents in many parts of the West and as we noted, Year Zero history became the official doctrine of the European Union[195].

In Germany, the desire to break free from the past has encouraged a complacent and conformist tendency that encourages sections of society to believe that they have left behind the bitter conflicts that frequently arose in the past. As one acute observer of the delusions and naivety shown particularly by young Germans towards historically rooted geopolitical questions noted, they have become 'intellectually and practically disarmed'. Ulrike Franke, a senior policy fellow at the European Council on Foreign Relations, noted that among her fellow German millennials, there is scepticism towards the legitimacy of geopolitics, an 'inability to think in terms of power and interest and a rejection of the military as an instrument of politics'[196].

Franke rightly associates the intellectual disarmament of young Germans with their loss of a sense of the past. 'We never felt as if we were a part of the ever-churning history, but rather, we had the impression of being outside of it,

194 http://webdoc.sub.gwdg.de/ebook/serien/p/ghi-dc/op20.pdf, p. 60.
195 See Furedi, F. (2018) *Populism And The European Culture Wars: The Conflict of Values between Hungary and the EU*, Routledge: London, pp. 89–93.
196 https://warontherocks.com/2021/05/a-millennial-considers-the-new-german-problem-after-30-years-of-peace/

born after the fact', she noted. Delusions about the end of history are often coupled with the prejudice that the nation and national interests have become irrelevant. The rejection of the salience of national interest has led to 'an almost romantic idea of international relations'. Franke observed that 'German millennials struggle with the military – specifically the idea that the military is an element of geopolitical power'. Writing eight months before the invasion of Ukraine, she stated that 'A higher number of millennials support reducing the German defence budget than any other age group, while support for a budgetary increase is lower among millennials than among all other groups'.

The low status that German society accorded to its military was demonstrated during the week leading up to the invasion of Ukraine. This sentiment is by no means confined to millennials. A lack of resolve to stand up to Russia was unambiguously communicated by the German Chancellor, Olaf Scholz. A few days before the invasion, he flew to Moscow to encourage a diplomatic resolution to the conflict. When he returned to Germany, he assumed the role of Putin's messenger. He urged the Ukrainian President, Volodymyr Zelensky, to accept Russian demands to negotiate over the so-called separatist republics in Donbas.[197] The supine stance adopted by the German Government was met with a sense of embarrassment by some of this nation's military leaders. Germany's highest-ranking military officer, Alfons Mais, went public to question his nation's army's combat readiness[198]. In a LinkedIn post, he wrote that the 'Bundeswehr, the army that I am privileged to lead, is more or less bare. The options that we can offer the politicians to support the alliance are extremely limited'. In a tone of frustration, he declared, 'we all saw it coming and were not able to get through with our arguments, to draw the conclusions from the Crimean annexation and implement them. This does not feel good! I am pissed off!'[199].

Germany's indifference to geopolitical interest is sometimes explained as the outcome of the fact that this nation's political establishment was riddled with guilt about its barbaric behaviour during the Second World War. No doubt, the horrors of the Second World War and particularly the memory of the Holocaust have encouraged this nation to adopt the image of the peaceful Good German. However, though Germany's attempt to escape from its past is more dramatic

---

197 https://www.telegraph.co.uk/news/2022/02/26/olaf-scholz-gave-vladimir-putin-green-light-invade/

198 https://www.foxnews.com/world/germany-army-standing-bare-limited-combat-readiness-top-chief

199 https://www.politico.eu/article/i-am-pissed-off-chief-of-the-german-army-alfons-mais-states/

than those of other societies, a similar pattern is evident throughout the Western world.

The lack of valuation for the affirmation of national interest is closely linked with the diminishing status enjoyed by historically patriotic values, such as duty and responsibility. Many Western commentators who find the heroism and resistance of Ukrainian people difficult to grasp are probably asking the question 'if attacked would our people put up such a fight? The post-nationalist philosopher, Jürgen Habermas, personifies the post-heroic mentality that prevails in his society. He contrasted the 'widely admired, heroic resistance and self-evident willingness to sacrifice displayed by the Ukrainian population with what might be expected of "our", generally speaking, Western European populations in a similar situation'[200]. He has clearly imbued what he characterises as the 'post-heroic mentality' that developed in Western Europe and appeared to resent the failure of Ukraine to empathise with Germany's reluctance to stop buying oil from Russia[201].

Anyone familiar with history would not be surprised that the 'post-heroic' attitudes that influence Western society remain alien to nations fighting to retain their independence. People with a cause to fight for long for heroes. Not so long ago, the ideals of fighting for a cause and even risking death attracted millions of young people to their nation's cause. Today, for many intellectuals, it is unthinkable that a significant section of society could find meaning in war. As Christopher Coker explained in his *Waging War Without Warriors?* wars have become detached from the values that influence everyday life. Wars like the so-called war against terrorism are not a cause but a policy conducted for pragmatic reasons[202]. In contrast to the celebration of heroic death by romantic intellectuals in 1914, today the loss of life in combat is regarded as a 'futile waste' with little meaning

Instead of glorifying heroism, the ethos of risk aversion has become institutionalised within the military. British Army commanders now have to draw up risk assessments for every aspect of their soldiers' training. General Sir Michael Rose, former head of the SAS, has spoken out about the destructive impact of

---

200 https://www.resetdoc.org/story/jurgen-habermas-war-indignation-west-red-line-dilemma/
201 This pont is well observed by Slavoj Žižek in https://www.project-syndicate.org/onpoint/
european-response-to-ukraine-war-test-for-climate-other-crises-by-slavoj-zizek-2022-05?utm_
source=Project+Syndicate+Newsletter&utm_campaign=d26a7ed864-covid_newsletter_05_11_
2022&utm_medium=email&utm_term=0_73bad5b7d8-d26a7ed864-104993029&mc_cid=
d26a7ed864&mc_eid=3ff8ccdea0
202 Coker, C. (2002.) *Waging war without warriors?: The changing culture of military conflict.*
Lynne Rienner Publishers: Boulder, CO.

risk-aversion and the ethos of safety on the morale of the British military. He has denounced the 'moral cowardice' that has encouraged what he describes as the 'most catastrophic collapse' of military ethos in recent history[203]. His statement was made almost 15 years before the West's humiliating withdrawal and abandonment of Afghanistan.

In November 2018, the then chief of the defence staff, General Sir Nick Carter, stated that he was worried about whether young people understood 'the notion of service'[204]. He seemed far from certain whether the young could be relied upon to support the military in the future. He suggested that something has gone seriously wrong in the way the young are educated and socialised. No doubt something has gone seriously wrong when society cannot cultivate a sense of loyalty and duty in the young.

Within the institutions of the British State, historically significant ideals of loyalty, duty and patriotism have given way to values associated with the cultural politics of identity. Even supposedly hard-core institutions like the Ministry of Defence have fallen prey to the fashionable fads associated with identity politics. MoD staff are advised to be careful about using the word 'female' in case it offends members of the trans community. Staff working for the MoD have also been encouraged to publicise their preferred pronouns[205].

As Russia invaded Ukraine, sections of the MoD appeared to be more interested in exploring their sexuality and gender identity than focusing on devising a strategy for containing military aggression[206]. During the days following the invasion of Russia, a campaign launched by British soldiers calling for the introduction of vegan uniforms illustrated the bizarre sense of priorities at work in the army[207]. Confronted with the infantilised behaviour of these soldiers, one is reminded of warning issues by the Roman political philosopher Cicero when he stated, 'to remain ignorant of history is to remain forever a child'.

The issue at stake is not simply the distraction from geopolitical realities associated with obsessions about pronouns, but the difficulty Western society has in giving meaning to its historical interests. The ideals of patriotism, courage, loyalty and duty have been side lined, in part, because they are associated

---

203 'J'Accuse! Top General lambasts "moral cowardice" of government and military chiefs', *The Daily Mail*, 12 April 2007.
204 https://www.thetimes.co.uk/article/young-cannot-be-relied-on-to-back-notion-of-service-says-general-sir-nick-carter-ptsOc6pkx
205 https://www.thetimes.co.uk/article/mod-tells-staff-to-state-name-rank-and-gender-pronoun-rcbwcrw5r
206 https://www.spiked-online.com/2022/02/25/the-security-services-have-gone-woke/
207 https://www.telegraph.co.uk/news/2022/02/27/soldiers-call-vegan-uniforms/

with the past. One of the consequences of the decades-long tendency to devalue historical consciousness is to erode the salience of the necessary values for preparing society to deal with a world where conflict is integral to people's lives.

Western military society's cultural estrangement from sacrifice is reflected through the institutionalisation of aversion to casualties. American military doctrine has become drawn towards the strategy of relying on technology to avoid casualties. The so-called Revolution in Military Affairs (RMA) can be seen as an attempt to avoid committing troops to a protracted and bloody encounter. According to one study, many 'statesman and generals believe, with absolute and unquestioning conviction, that the United States can no longer use force successfully unless American military casualties are virtually nil'[208]. The main merit of the frequent use of unmanned drone strikes for the Obama and the Trump administrations was that it avoided casualties to American military personnel. The risk-averse and post-heroic military doctrine was fully at work during America's humiliating defeat and withdrawal from Afghanistan. One analyst believes that risk-aversion has undermined the very effectiveness of the American army: 'As the emphasis on risk avoidance filters down the chain of command, junior commanders and their soldiers become aware that low-risk behaviour is expected and act accordingly.[209]'

A sense of historical amnesia deprives Western culture of the power of the memory that many of its youth stood ready and died in battle not so long ago. Writing in the early stages of the First World War, the renowned German sociologist Max Weber declared that a community of solidarity created on the battlefield provided meaning and motivation comparable to the experience of religious brotherhood. He stated that a 'war does something to a warrior which, in its concrete meaning, is unique', because 'it makes him experience a consecrated meaning of death which is characteristic only of death in war'. Unlike normal death, which, in a modern secular world, has no special meaning, in war and 'only in war, the individual can *believe* that he knows he is dying "for" something'[210]. Weber's sacralisation of an individual's sacrifice of life was not simply wishful propaganda. His claim regarding the 'the very extraordinary quality of brotherliness of war, and of death in war' still had meaning for many soldiers

208 Mueller, J.E. (2006) *Overblown: How politicians and the terrorism industry inflate national security threats, and why we believe them.* Simon and Schuster: New York, p. 12.

209 Lacquement Jr, R.A. (2004) 'The Casual-Aversion Myth', *Naval War College Review*, vol. 57, no. 1, p. 41.

210 Weber, M. (1915) 'Religious rejections of the world and their directions' in Gerth, H. H. and Wright Mills, C. W. (eds.) (1958) *From Max Weber: Essays in Sociology*, Galaxy Books: New York, p. 335.

– from all sides – who had volunteered to fight in this War. As the experience of Ukraine demonstrates, the belief that one is fighting and potentially dying for something still motivates and inspires millions of people who value the preservation of their nation and way of life.

In recent times Western society has become sceptical of the value of courage and heroism. It is through the prism of scepticism that it perceives the events of the past. Moreover, historical amnesia encourages society to attach contemporary precautionary values to the past. Reading history backwards, the ethos of precaution projects back into the past present-day concerns. It conveys cynicism towards readings of the past, which celebrate episodes of heroism and courageous behaviour. The claim that risk and casualty aversion of today is an eternal fact of life is frequently recycled through anachronistic versions of history. There is a discernible tendency toward 'debunking' historical narratives that allude to heroic deeds and acts of altruistic sacrifice and deconstructing the meaning of long-cherished values, such as courage, heroism and loyalty. As Bill Durodié noted: 'Henry V's decisive defeat of the French at Agincourt in 1415, as well as Shakespeare's account of it with the infamous 'band of brothers', can now be portrayed as being about people suffering from 'a centuries-old "deception" about the glory of war'[211].

Heroism is often mocked or dismissed as implausible. A new genre of popular culture and historical narratives is devoted to exposing the sordid 'secret lives' of past heroes. Claims of heroism are countered with disparagement and scorn. At best, they are depicted as flawed characters; at worst, they are condemned as power-hungry frauds. As Michiko Kakutani, the former literary critic of the *New York Times,* remarked, 'formerly we used to canonise our heroes', but the 'modern method is to vulgarise them'. Kakutani argues that biography has turned into a blood sport, committed mercilessly to debunking its subject[212]. Bringing heroes down to earth comes instinctively to a culture that finds duty, sacrifice or risk-taking alien to its nature. In numerous accounts, heroism is dismissed as an old fashioned and even offensive trait. As Christopher Coker remarks in his book, *The Warrior Ethos,* 'we tend to deprive' heroes 'of the fullness of their lives in order to support and sustain the smallness of our own'[213].

When confronted with the prospect of war, there are some very difficult decisions to be made. Taking history seriously is essential for understanding the

---

211 See Bill Durodié 'Death of the Warrior Ethos', http://www.durodie.net/index.php/site/printable/94/

212 M. Kakutani, 'Critic's Notebook: Biography becomes blood sport', *The New York Times*, 20 May 1994.

213 Coker, C. (2007) *The Warrior Ethos*, Routledge; London, p. 3.

issues at stake. As Slavoj Žižek noted in response to Western Europe's risk-averse response to the war in Ukraine, 'unfortunately, "heroic" acts will be needed again'. He dismisses the 'comfortable, non-heroic complacency' that characterises contemporary Western European society[214]. The West would do well to recover the historical ideals that underpin a militant culture of democracy. Otherwise, while it is playing with pronouns, Rome will burn.

---

214 https://www.project-syndicate.org/onpoint/european-response-to-ukraine-war-test-for-cli
mate-other-crises-by-slavoj-zizek-2022-05?utm_source=Project+Syndicate+Newsletter&utm_cam
paign=d26a7ed864-covid_newsletter_05_11_2022&utm_medium=email&utm_term=0_
73bad5b7d8-d26a7ed864-104993029&mc_cid=d26a7ed864&mc_eid=3ff8ccdea0

Chapter 5
Ukraine – A Focus for Moral Redemption

It is now widely acknowledged that the war in Ukraine has destabilised the pre-existing distribution of global power. It represents a pivotal moment in global affairs, with previous assumptions about the running of the world order now called into question. The invasion of Ukraine has set in motion forces that enhance global insecurity and are likely to intensify rivalries between nations and blocs. The emergence of a new geopolitical landscape questions the dominant theories and ideas through which international relations were interpreted in the post-Cold War era. Suddenly the ideology of globalisation stands exposed as a fantasy dogma contradicted by the reality of a world of nations. Yet again, great power competition has acquired an ominous form, and the issue of national security is once more on top of the policy agenda.

Events in Ukraine have not only called into question the survival of existing geopolitical arrangements but also brought to the surface deep-rooted intellectual and moral crisis of the West. Almost overnight, the Western political establishment has been forced to acknowledge that history actually exists, and that it actually matters. 'History is brutally back, and Ukraine will test Europe's appetite for the consequences' observes the Dutch historian Luuk van Middelaar[215].

All this is happening at a time when the West is internally divided on matters of culture and moral norms. 'The second American civil war is already happening' notes Robert Reich.[216] This culture war has divided America to the point that its two sides inhabit a different moral universe. A disunited home front invariably has disturbing implications for the defence of national security.

The moral disorientation that prevails in the West is not unconnected to its loss of the sense of the past. Historical amnesia acquired an institutional expression when Western societies sought to distance themselves from their traditions. This escape from the past coincided with a flight from the nation and its traditions. Traditional national security concerns were increasingly disparaged precisely because they were *traditional* and because of this were, supposedly, far less relevant in a globalised setting where a growing proportion of decision-making was outsourced to transnational institutions. Amongst the cultural elites and

215 https://www.theguardian.com/world/commentisfree/2022/mar/09/history-brutally-back-ukraine-europes-appetite-nuclear-superpower
216 https://www.theguardian.com/commentisfree/2022/may/11/second-american-civil-war-robert-reich

https://doi.org/10.1515/9783110981544-007

sections of the political establishment, the pursuit of national interest was frequently depicted as an echo of the past.

In the post-Cold War era, the devaluation of sovereignty acquired a hegemonic influence amongst mainstream international relations academics and commentators and experts working in the NGO sector. In these decades, anti-national prejudice often masqueraded as objective academic analysis. The principle of sovereignty was derided on the ground that its exercise was bound to be ineffective in the era of globalisation. Sovereignty was frequently coupled with the word 'myth'. Many asserted that the nation-state could not resist the forces of globalisation. Others diagnosed the demise of the nation-state and declared that domestic politics had become pointless. 'After decades of globalisation, our political system, become obsolete', claimed the author Rana Dasgupta[217]. This attitude continued to prevail during the Covid pandemic when some argued that the virus did not recognise borders and that national governments were helpless to deal with this problem[218]. Yet the experience of the pandemic demonstrated that, in the end, people's access to health care and vaccination depended on their own governments, rather than on transnational institutions, such as the World Health Organisation. In the end, the lesson drawn by millions of people was that a global threat to world health, such as the coronavirus, could only be effectively contained by the national actions of sovereign states.

Critics of sovereignty often idealise a borderless, abstract, human rights-based vision of world affairs that 'transcends' national interest. Others argue that the problems of the 21st century are global in character and thus require global solutions. From this standpoint, it is often argued that national governments only get in the way of international nongovernmental organisations (NGOs) trying to do the right thing.

The growth in influence of transnational thinking has run in parallel with the de-nationalisation of sections of the Western elites. Superficially, the trend towards the de-nationalisation of the elites appears to be the outcome of globalisation. Numerous commentators have argued that as global networks displace national ones, supra-national institutions attract the best brains. Entrepreneurs, scientists and academics have begun to orientate their thinking more and more globally and adopt a casual orientation towards their national affiliation.

However, the de-nationalisation of the elites is not simply driven by globalisation. Politically and culturally, they feel estranged from their national institu-

---

217 https://www.theguardian.com/news/2018/apr/05/demise-of-the-nation-state-rana-das gupta

218 https://www.friendsofeurope.org/insights/coronavirus-has-shattered-many-long-held-myths-about-globalisation

tions and affiliations. They often convey the belief that these institutions are out-dated products of a past that is radically different to their world. They find it eas-ier to get things done through international institutions and networks. Thus, be-fore Brexit, many English Members of the European Parliament (MEPs) felt they had more in common with a French colleague who was a fellow member of the MEP club than with the voters who elected them. This sensibility is enhanced by the fact that within their nation, the cultural elites live a detached life from those of less fortunate citizens. One of the first commentators to draw attention to the trend toward the denationalisation of the elites was the American political phi-losopher, Christopher Lasch. He wrote in 1995:

> 'Those who covet membership in the new aristocracy of brains tend to congregate on the coast, turning their back on the heartland and cultivating ties with the international market in fast-moving money, glamour, fashion, and popular culture. It is a question whether they think of themselves as Americans at all. Patriotism, certainly, does not rank very high in their hierarchy of virtues'[219].

Lasch noted that in contrast to their lack of enthusiasm for patriotism, they read-ily embraced multiculturalism and diversity.

Through the medium of the culture wars, the detachment of the elites from the life of a nation has become intensified. From their perspective, they feel clos-er to their transnational friends than to fellow citizens 'who do not think like us'. Since the 1990s, the psychic distance between the elite outlook and national sen-sibilities has widened. Drawn towards different brands of the politics of lifestyle and identity, members of the cultural elite regard their national identity as no big deal. Those charged with the conduct of international affairs and foreign policy often share the cultural outlook of their peers in the political establishment. Since their sensibility is more sympathetic to the transnational than the national and the regional, their behaviour as geopolitical actors often lacks clarity. And in some circumstances, it is unpredictable and confused. The tragic consequence of half-baked humanitarian intervention in Syria in 2014 is testimony to the mess created by diplomacy that finds it difficult to distinguish between transnational cultural rhetoric and national interest.

The outcome is always unpredictable when diplomacy and geopolitics be-come entwined with cultural politics and identity affiliations. The polarised po-litical landscape created by cultural conflict within the domestic sphere is bad enough. But when it becomes internationalised and draws in foreign actors, its consequences can be far more destabilising and explosive.

---

219 Lasch, C. (1995), *Revolt of the Elites: And The Betrayal of Democracy*, WW Norton: New York.

The estrangement of sections of the Western political establishment from the ideal of national interest partly explains its lack of clarity and ability to engage with the challenge posed by foreign adversaries. Certainly, the elites of Western societies today appear to be far less effective than their counterparts in the 1950s and 1960s. Some observers contend that elites are increasingly fragmented and lack the capacity to exercise leadership. Elite fragmentation means that often it is unable to act effectively[220]. This development is particularly striking in relation to the United States, where the government is often paralysed in a self-inflicted gridlock. Humiliating setbacks in Afghanistan, Syria, Iraq and Libya suggest that the so-called power elite is conspicuously unable to exercise its power effectively. As the historian Richard Lachmann pointed out:

'America is unique among the world's dominant powers of the past five hundred years in its repeated failure to achieve military objectives over decades. Those failures are even more extraordinary because they occurred in the absence of a rising military rival'[221].

The absence of a 'rising military rival' suggests that repeated failures in foreign policy are not due to the strength of the adversary but due to the outcome of fundamental problems rooted in the outlook, values and practices of the American political and military establishment. Indeed, it seems evident that it is the weak normative foundation for the exercise of elite power, which has led to the absence of a *l'esprit de corps* and a sense of legitimacy that has played a decisive role in the foreign affair failures of the West. Lachmann's closely argued study of the ineffectiveness of the international projection of American power raises questions that we might ask in relation to similar problems in the Western world, such as unsuccessful initiatives in the domain of drug control, education or social integration.

Most explanations for the weakening of elite cohesion and its inability to formulate an authoritative shared outlook focus on the economic and social changes that became evident during the late 1970s. These developments – deregulation, financialisation and the rise of digital technology – clearly contributed to the disruption of institutions, the erosion of institutional loyalties and the loss of institutional memory. However, there were other, arguably more important factors, at work. These elements are best understood as the outward manifestations of the historic problem of elite legitimation – a problem that was exacerbated by

220 Mizruchi, M.S., and Hyman, M. (2014) 'Elite fragmentation and the decline of the United States', *Political Power and Social Theory*, vol. 26.
221 Lachmann, R. (2020) *First-Class Passengers on a Sinking Ship: Elite Politics and the Decline of Great Powers*, Verso: London, p. 4.

a loss of conviction in the values and outlook into which previous generations of elites were socialised.

It is my contention that the confusions that both lead to and are amplified by historical amnesia create the condition where the capacity to give meaning to events becomes diminished. The loss of a sense of the past has deprived the ruling classes of the confidence that comes with knowing your place in the world. This leads to their equivocation about what values to uphold and defend. Moreover, the combination of a de-territorialised and denationalised sensibility works to destabilise the process of decision making in the domain of foreign affairs.

Without greater clarity about its position and authority, the elites find it difficult to endow power with meaning. Zaki Laïdi clearly articulated this point in his important study, *A World Without Meaning: The Crisis Of Meaning In International Politics* (1998), when he wrote that '*Power is nothing when it has lost meaning*'[222]. From Vietnam to Afghanistan, experience indicates that those attempting to exercise power who are unable to draw on moral resources are sooner or later confronted with the spectre of humiliation. Laïdi's emphasis on the problem of meaning highlights the loss of moral clarity, which in turn, has served to diminish the capacity to make judgement calls.

If the ruling elites of the West struggle to know what they stand for, it is understandable that the rest of society is also at a loss to understand what values to uphold. The precondition for the public's support for foreign and defence policies is that it believes that there is something worth fighting for. Historically people have been prepared to confront violent threats to their lives and make heroic sacrifices if a conflict had an important meaning for them. That is why wars are not simply about military action. They also involve a battle of ideas. The problem of meaning discussed above finds its clearest expression in the West's difficulty in expressing what it stands for and engaging in the battle for hearts and minds. Confusions about what the West stands for have undermined its geopolitical literacy. Some analysts have even gone so far as to assert that even the police force and intelligence gathering agencies are influenced by a mood of 'Western self-loathing', which undermines their operational judgment.[223]

The war in Ukraine brings into relief the fragile state of the moral authority of Western politicians. At the same time, it is regarded by many of them as a cause through which they can revitalise a sense of legitimacy. This is the first time since the end of the Cold War that it appears that there is a cause through

---

222 Laïdi (1998).
223 Neumann, P., and Smith, M.L.R, (2005) 'Missing the plot? Intelligence and discourse failure', *Orbis*, vol. 49, no. 1, p. 100.

which many policymakers believe that the West could reinvent itself as a self-confident and convincing moral agent. In contrast to the moral climate prevailing in their societies, it appears to sections of the Western ruling classes as if the classical virtues that have inspired people over the centuries are still alive and flourishing on the battlefield of Ukraine. As the veteran business and economics columnist for the *New York Times*, Peter Coy noted, 'Courage seemed to be dead. Then came Zelensky'[224]. Coy reminded his readers that:

'Courage can seem like an outdated virtue in a world of selfish genes and utilitarian economics. If we are meant to put ourselves first—to maximize our individual utility—then what room is left for heroism? How can a self be selfless? It sounds almost illogical.'

However, Coy, like many of his colleagues in the Western media, politicians and policymakers, have finally found a hero who has reminded them that courage is not entirely a lost cause. 'Volodymyr Zelensky, the president of Ukraine, has reminded us that courage is not out of date', observed Coy.

Numerous commentators are drawn to the moral authority enjoyed by the cause of Ukraine and its president, Volodymyr Zelensky. They frequently suggest that 'Zelensky has a unique combination of moral authority and uncensored authenticity that has helped rally the West around him'[225]. They point to his 'sound and statesmanlike' behaviour. According to John Herbst, the senior director of the Atlantic Council's Eurasia Center and former U.S. ambassador to Ukraine, 'at the core of Zelenskyy's success has been the moral authority he carries in the face of the Russian invasion'[226].

At a time when many Western societies have become culturally divided and when values associated with the West have become a target of contestation, Ukraine has unexpectedly emerged as a cause that many believe can assist it in regaining moral clarity. As *New York Times* columnist David Brooks put it:

'I have faith in the ideas and the moral systems that we have inherited. What we call "the West" is not an ethnic designation or an elitist country club. The heroes of Ukraine are showing that at its best, it is a moral accomplishment, and unlike its rivals, it aspires to extend dignity, human rights and self-determination to all'[227].

224 https://www.nytimes.com/2022/05/13/opinion/courage-heroism-economics.html

225 https://www.politico.com/news/2022/03/16/zelenskyy-congress-ukraine-russia-00017548

226 https://abcnews.go.com/International/comedian-wartime-leader-zelenskyy-helping-ukraine-win-information/story?id=84340282

227 https://www.nytimes.com/2022/04/08/opinion/globalization-global-culture-war.html.

In this instance, faith in 'the West' is validated by the 'heroes of Ukraine'. This is why flying Ukraine's flag serves as a medium for symbolising moral authority. The unprecedented display of support for Ukraine by Western societies in the aftermath of its invasion is not motivated simply by the understandable impulse to support a nation fighting for survival against the odds. Western gestures of support are also prompted by the self-serving impulse of regarding events in Ukraine as a resource for moral redemption.

Me! Me! Me! Culture Discovers Itself in Ukraine

One of the least attractive features of the Western response to Russia's invasion of Ukraine is its narcissistic tendency to insert itself and its feelings into its narrative about the war. Listening to the BBC's *Today* Programme and to other media outlets, it is difficult to avoid the impression that 'it is all about me'. Time and again, the interviewer poses the predictable question 'how do you feel?'. People are asked about their motives and emotional feelings, for example, about providing refugees a home.

Hosting a refugee in your home is promoted on the grounds that it can be a life-changing experience. According to a commentator in *The Conversation:*

> 'Hosting is also an investment and enrichment for the host's own lives. The hosts in our studies show that as months go by they feel a great sense of connection and companionship, with many stating they had found "friends for life". For those who had children in the household, they found that their children's eyes had been opened to a whole new world, learning a new language and culture and becoming more tolerant of those who are different from them'[228].

What's at stake with this advice is not merely an appeal to the self-interest of the host but an encouragement to perceive the crisis in Ukraine as a life-changing experience. This focus on supposed therapeutic benefits instrumentalises what should be an act of solidarity.

The narcissistic culture of the West has encouraged the personalisation of the war in Ukraine. This tendency assumes a grotesque manifestation in the higher education sector, where mental health entrepreneurs incite students and staff to perceive themselves as at-risk emotionally by exposure to media depictions of the war. The University of British Columbia in Canada invites 'stu-

---

228 https://theconversation.com/thinking-of-welcoming-a-ukrainian-refugee-into-your-home-our-research-can-help-you-be-a-good-host-179212

dents of any background who have been affected by the war in Ukraine' to 'come listen and share their experiences'[229]. John Hopkins University offers 'well-being resources' for students 'affected by Russia's invasion of Ukraine'. Its message to students is that 'we hope that at a personal level, you are taking good care of yourself and making use of every resource available to you to navigate these difficult and uncertain times'[230]. It is as if John Hopkins imagines that it is located in Kyiv and its American students are sharing the pain of their peers in Ukraine.

A statement issued by Newcastle University's Sabbatical Officers illustrates how British students are expected to emotionally internalise the tragedy unfolding in Ukraine. It notes that 'we, like many of you feel helpless in this situation' and that 'we are aware that our students may also be affected by these events and that this is a deeply troubling and difficult time for them and those close to them'. Undergraduates are reminded that the students' union is a 'safe space which welcomes all students'[231].

There was something truly performative about the provision of a safe space for British students who are 'affected' by the war at a time when hundreds of thousands of Ukrainian refugees are fleeing for their lives. However, even more disturbing is the impulse to transform Ukraine into a brand through which people can cultivate their identity and attempt to advertise their moral status. The rock star Bono is paradigmatic in this respect. To demonstrate that he is a genuine 'thought-leader' who carries the weight of the suffering of Ukraine on his shoulders, Bono wrote a poem that cast the Prime Minister of Ukraine, Zelensky, into the role of St Patrick. For him, the suffering of Ukraine and Ireland were depicted as interchangeable:

And they struggle for us to be free
From the psycho in this human family
Ireland's sorrow and pain
Is now the Ukraine
And St Patrick's name now Zelensky.[232]

229 https://grad-postdoc.med.ubc.ca/support-and-resources-for-students-and-staff-affected-by-the-war-in-ukrain
230 https://wellbeing.jhu.edu/well-being-resources-for-students-affected-by-russias-invasion-of-ukraine
231 https://www.nusu.co.uk/news/article/7710/A-statement-from-your-Sabbatical-Officer-team
232 https://www.theguardian.com/us-news/2022/mar/17/nancy-pelosi-bono-poem-st-patricks-day-ukraine

The American politician Nancy Pelosi, speaker of the U.S. House of Representatives, decided to recite the poem during the marking of St Patrick's Day at the annual Friends of Ireland lunch in Washington, DC.

Predictably Bono took the first opportunity available to a fly to Ukraine to record a video of him singing with a soldier in the Kyiv metro station

Following Bono, numerous attention-seeking celebrities sought to brand themselves by appropriating the colour of Ukraine's flag. Actress AnnaLynne McCord also discovered her poetic voice. She posted a video of herself reading a totally weird two-minute poem addressed to Putin. In this poem, she communicates the claim that she understands the emotional pain that drove the Russian president to invade Ukraine[233]. Assuming the role of a nourishing and emotionally literate earth-mother, McCord cast herself into a leading role in the drama, without a shred of self-consciousness.

Narcissistic virtue signalling assumes a more ominous tone when it is promoted by politically motivated members of the Western establishment who regard the war as an opportunity to rehabilitate the West morally. Media commentators and policymakers are quite explicit in representing the war in Ukraine as a medium for the revival of the West. As an editorial in London-based *Daily Telegraph* put it, 'Britain led on Ukraine. Now it must lead the fight to revive the West.'[234] According to the editorial, Russia's invasion has 'created a stark new philosophical contest between authoritarianism and freedom'. For many, the 'stark' contrast between good and evil represents an opportunity for moral redemption.

The American writer Kori Schake believes that Putin has inadvertently 'revitalised the West's liberal order'[235]. Putin is the accidental architect of the West's revitalisation.

The most enthusiastic practitioners of utilising the experience of Ukraine for moral revival are to be found in the ranks of the supporters of the project of the EU. The EU faces an unprecedented crisis of legitimacy, and many of its leaders are acutely sensitive to their lack of moral authority. To limit the damage caused by their unpopularity in many parts of Europe, its Parliament decided in April 2022 to create a 'common curriculum' for insulating children from the scourge

233 https://pagesix.com/2022/02/24/annalynne-mccord-trolled-over-putin-video-amid-russia-ukraine-war/?_ga=2.104652992.1302736414.1645548913-1901699925.1630619251

234 https://www.telegraph.co.uk/opinion/2022/03/06/britain-led-ukraine-now-must-lead-fight-revive-west

235 https://www.theatlantic.com/international/archive/2022/02/vladimir-putin-ukraine-invasion-liberal-order/622950

of Euroscepticism[236]. From the standpoint of many advocates of the EU, the war in Ukraine has come along as a godsend. 'Ukraine has unified the EU like never before by giving it a renewed sense of purpose', wrote Paul Grod for the Atlantic Council[237].

Numerous commentators argue that Ukraine is helping Europe 'go back to its values'. 'Put simply, the European Union needs Ukraine,' wrote Grod, before adding that it needs Ukraine to 'demonstrate its own commitment to European values'[238]. Ukraine's struggle for its national independence is regularly presented as a crusade for promoting EU values. Writing in this vein, Timothy Garton Ash of the *Guardian* claimed that 'Zelensky and his people are fighting for their lives to defend European values'[239]. His point was echoed by European Commission Vice-President Maros Sefcovic, who, supporting a Ukrainian bid for EU membership, stated that Ukrainians are 'dying for European values ... we want them in'[240]. Through promoting Ukraine as an advert for the legitimacy of the EU and its values, a bitter and bloody struggle for national survival is transformed into a public relations exercise for an institution in search of legitimacy.

There is more than a hint of opportunism in security expert Benjamin Tallis' advocacy of granting EU membership to Ukraine. Tallis, a fellow at the Hertie School's Centre for International Security in Berlin, argues that; 'In recent years we have lost our way. Integrating Ukraine could help us find it again— and rediscover the EU's ability to genuinely provide security for Europeans'[241].

To his credit, at least Tallis acknowledges the fact that the EU has lost its way and therefore needs an external agency to help revitalise it. However, this acknowledgement overlooks the question: what is there to revitalise? The Europe of values to which commentators like Garton Ash refer are conspicuously absent within the institutions of the EU. As I have argued elsewhere, the leaders of the EU have detached themselves from the moral legacy and historic values of Europe[242]. However, they have not been able to elaborate an alternative system of values with which to legitimate its institutions. Jacques Delors, the former

---

236 https://www.telegraph.co.uk/world-news/2022/04/16/eu-accused-indoctrinating-children-meps-back-europe-wide-compulsory

237 https://www.atlanticcouncil.org/blogs/ukrainealert/the-eu-needs-ukraine

238 https://www.atlanticcouncil.org/blogs/ukrainealert/the-eu-needs-ukraine

239 https://www.theguardian.com/commentisfree/2022/mar/04/ukraine-eu-membership-zelenskiy-european-values-war

240 https://www.france24.com/en/tv-shows/the-interview/20220304-ukrainians-are-dying-for-european-values-we-want-them-in-eu-s-sefcovic

241 https://ip-quarterly.com/en/integrating-ukraine-can-help-eu-find-its-way-again

242 Furedi (2018), chapter 1.

president of the European Commission, recognised this problem when he drew attention to the EU's reluctance to engage with this problem openly. In 2010, he stated that 'today we have hidden our shared values'. In this remarkable statement, Delors explicitly criticised the leadership of the EU for 'hiding' Europe's shared values. Delors argued that the failure to uphold Europe's values by the EU's political elite would have drastic consequences in the future. He asserted:

'I do not know where the frontiers of this Europe of values are to be found but, from an intellectual viewpoint, European society does exist, even though today we have hidden our shared values. We have done so on the one hand because we are terrified by globalisation and, on the other, because we are developing a kind of individualism that is made worse by a world characterized by media coverage and a kind of politics based on public opinion polls. All those values that go to make up a society are being done away with; day after day they are being destroyed. If the values of Europe are in decline, then it is Europe that suffers.'[243]

Delors' concern about the apparent indifference of political leaders to Europe's shared historical values was particularly directed at the casual manner with which they ignored the cultural legacy of the continent's past. It is unlikely that Ukraine can make up for the EU's value deficit. Nevertheless, the fantasy that the war in Ukraine could revitalise the EU continues to influence its hopeful policymakers.

It is not simply EU bureaucrats but also Anglo-American liberals who regard Ukraine as their potential saviour. 'This war can save liberalism' argues Francis Fukuyama[244]. Fukuyama, who regards the American version of liberal democracy as the high point of human civilisation, has been disappointed and worried about its failure to endow public life with meaning in recent years. Since the Cold War, American liberal democracy has lost its way. Unable to acknowledge its lack of moral and intellectual resources, it has blamed 'populism' for all its troubles. However, now Putin has provided it with an opportunity for moral rehabilitation. It hopes that a new sense of unity can be forged by standing up to the new version of the evil empire. As Fukuyama explained, 'with this invasion of another democratic country, Putin has created a certain amount of moral clarity'[245]. What Fukuyama means by this statement is that 'as against Putin and his corrupt oligarchs we look quite good'. 'We'll take that', argues Fukuyama and

---

243 See Tietze, N., and Bielefeld, U. 'An interview with Jacques Delors', *Mittelweg* 36, 8 September 2010, published by *Eurozine:* https://www.eurozine.com/in-search-of-europe/
244 https://unherd.com/2022/03/this-war-can-save-liberalism
245 https://unherd.com/2022/03/this-war-can-save-liberalism

members of the Anglo-American foreign policy establishment. However, relying on a moral contrast with Putin to gain clarity is unlikely to provide liberal democracy or the West with a durable form of legitimacy.

Fukuyama believes that the West could recover its loss of confidence in itself because of Ukraine's military success against Russia. Carried away by Ukraine's successes on the battlefield, he speculated about the possibility of Russia's outright defeat:

> 'The collapse of ... [Russia's] ... position could be sudden and catastrophic, rather than happening slowly through a war of attrition. The army in the field will reach a point where it can neither be supplied nor withdrawn, and morale will vaporize. ... Putin will not survive the defeat of his army ... A Russian defeat will make possible a "new birth of freedom," and get us out of our funk about the declining state of global democracy. The spirit of 1989 will live on, thanks to a bunch of brave Ukrainians.'[246]

A 'bunch of brave Ukrainians' are ordained with the mission of redeeming the West.

Fukuyama's representation of Ukraine as the saviour of liberalism and freedom is connected to the belief that the negative example of Russia's behaviour and the setback suffered by Putin can be used to strike a blow against populism within the United States. That is why he predicted the imminent 'new birth of freedom' leading to the final defeat of populism[247]. From this perspective, the forces of populism in the U.S, and Putin are connected so that the defeat of the latter would represent a major setback to the former. For Fukuyama, the defeat of Russia would mean defeating Trump and his supporters. In another interview he concluded:

> 'The war in Ukraine impacts the American people in the sense that, if Vladimir Putin succeeds, then such people here—those anti-democratic forces—will succeed as well. I believe they actually pose a real and present danger to American democracy, and if they're not beaten back we could be facing a serious constitutional crisis in this country in 2024. It is all connected.'[248]

From this perspective, Ukraine is as much a domestic issue as an international one. Almost casually, Ukraine is transformed into a sub-plot in the culture wars that so divides American society.

---

246 https://www.washingtonpost.com/opinions/2022/03/14/putin-could-lose-ukraine-fukuyama-optimistic

247 https://www.americanpurpose.com/blog/fukuyama/preparing-for-defeat

248 https://www.salon.com/2022/04/18/francis-fukuyama-on-putin-and-why-ukraine-is-key-to-saving-liberal-democracy

Ukraine has even been instrumentalised to support the cause of Scottish independence. 'Ukraine war bolsters the case for independence', argued Nicola Sturgeon, the first minister of Scotland[249]. The narcissistic manner with which different parties in the West have instrumentalised the invasion of Ukraine calls into question the durability of its support for this nation. There is something truly ethnocentric about how values that have a feeble existence in the West are revitalised through the bloody sacrifices of the people of Ukraine. When Ukraine becomes a medium for the pursuit of the moral rehabilitation of the West, it becomes evident that the culture of narcissism is not simply about individual celebrities attempting to insert themselves into the war. It is far more insidious than the behaviour of attention-seeking celebrities.

Gaining moral clarity from the tragic circumstances experienced by the people of Ukraine is a distasteful example of cultural parasitism. Those who seek moral clarity through exploiting the troubles of others are unlikely to gain any durable moral authority. Worse still, the practitioners of this 'all about me' approach to the war do a disservice to the people of Ukraine. It is unrealistic to expect the West to adopt policies based on altruism. There is nothing wrong with supporting Ukraine on the basis of national interest. However, policymaking that is informed by cultural narcissism tends to be incoherent, unstable and unreliable. The people of Ukraine deserve more than that. They deserve to be taken seriously on their own account. It is their story and not ours to hijack and make our own.

Moral Disarmament of the West

The quest for moral redemption through Ukraine suggests that the support for this nation's struggle is often subjected to an alien agenda.

As we hinted previously, events in Ukraine and the confusions about geopolitical matters sweeping the Western world are not unconnected to the forces of history unleashed during the early decades of the 20th century. The chain of events that followed in the wake of World War One continues to disrupt life in the 21st century. It is important to draw attention to an often-overlooked historical fact: the great wars of the 20th century were not simply motivated by geopolitical concerns. Domestic issues and ideological commitments intertwined with how national interests were affirmed on the field of battle. Domestic politics seam-

---

249 https://www.thetimes.co.uk/article/ukraine-war-bolsters-case-for-independence-insists-sturgeon-b90572tw2.

lessly intertwined with interstate relations[250]. Moreover, conflicts over values were embedded in the consciousness of many people who were motivated to fight a war. Idealism motivated millions. Subsequent disappointment regarding the failure to realise these ideals intensified a tendency toward a *zeitgeist* of pessimism and demoralisation, which periodically permeates the West. The gradual hardening of this trend over the decades would eventually lead to the crystallisation of the phenomenon of the *moral disarmament of the West.*[251]

The moral disarmament of the West is an indirect outcome of the Culture War that has been rumbling along since the interwar era[252]. The main target of the Culture War was the legacy of the past. It always sought to distance society from its past and, by implication, attempted to diminish the capacity of Western culture to think historically. During the interwar era, numerous thinkers became aware of this loss. Suddenly, the taken-for-granted assumptions about civilisation, progress and the nature of change lost their capacity to illuminate human experience. As the prominent English historian H.A.L. Fisher acknowledged in 1934, he could no longer discern in history the 'plot', the 'rhythm' and 'predetermined pattern' that appeared so obvious to observers in the past[253]. The cultural historian Paul Fussell claims that after the First World War, it is difficult if not impossible to imagine the future as the continuation of the past; 'the Great War was perhaps the last to be conceived as taking place within a seamless, purposeful "history" involving a coherent stream of time running from past to future'[254]. A dramatic shift in the Western world's sense of temporality had altered people's relationship to their past.

In his memoir, *My Early Life* (1930), Winston Churchill drew attention to the crisis of normativity, which he experienced as the estrangement of his society from the legacy and the values of the past. He observed:

'I wonder often whether any other generation has seen such astounding revolutions of data and values as those through which we have lived. Scarcely anything, material or establish-

250 Mayer, A.J. (1969) 'Internal Causes and Purposes of War in Europe, 1870–1956: A Research Assignment', *The Journal of Modern History*, vol. 41, no. 3, pp. 291–303.
251 For a discussion of moral disarmament in France during the interwar years in France, see Siegel, M.L. (2004) *The moral disarmament of France: education, pacifism, and patriotism, 1914–1940*, Cambridge University Press: Cambridge.
252 See Furedi (2021) for a discussion of the century long cultural conflict.
253 Cited in Eksteins, M. (1989) *Rites of Spring: The Great War and the Birth of the Modern Age*, Houghton Mifflin: Boston, p. 291.
254 Fussell, P. (1975) *The Great War and Modern memory*, Oxford University Press: Oxford, p. 21.

ed, which I was brought up to believe was permanent and vital, has lasted. Everything I was sure or was taught to be sure, was impossible has happened.'[255]

Lord Eustace Perry echoed Churchill when he wrote in 1934 that there was 'no natural idea in which we any longer believe'. He added that 'we have lost the easy self-confidence which distinguished our Victorian grandfathers'[256]. It was as if sections of the British establishment had unwittingly abandoned the normative foundation of their way of life.

The loss of that 'easy self-confidence' to which Perry referred would, during the decades to come, mutate into a crisis of moral authority. As Western societies detached themselves from their past, they became less and less identified with the values associated with their historical legacy. The weakening attachment to the historical community – especially that of the nation-state – deprived the West of the moral resources on which it could draw for guidance. In a pessimistic vein, Arendt stressed that one of the most significant outcomes of this development was that the very idea of authority had become a lost cause. In an essay published in 1958, 'What was authority?', she went so far as to refer to this phenomenon in the past tense.[257]

In the domain of public life, one of the most remarkable symptoms of the moral disarmament of the West was its growing indifference to the authority of the nation-state. The downsizing of the nation-state and its role in global affairs was not simply a direct response to globalisation but also a loss of identification with its authority. As Andrew Michta observed, it was the erosion of the authoritative status of the nation state and its central role in global affairs that 'lies at the base of the deepening political crisis in Western democracies'[258]. Interconnected with this consensus was a constellation of civic virtues – patriotism, duty, service – whose status today are less and less validated by the dominant institutions of society. Typically, diminishing the status of civic virtues deprives society's elites of the sense of purpose required to guide society effectively.

The moral disarmament of the West acquired its most striking expression in the sphere of socialisation and public education[259]. Many educators self-con-

---

255 Churchill, W. (1930) *My Early Life*, Thornton Butterworth Limited: London, p. 87.

256 Cited in Rich, P. (1989) 'Imperial Decline and the resurgence of British national identity' in Kushner, T., and Lunn, K. (eds.) (1989) *Traditions of Intolerance*, Manchester University Press: Manchester, p. 65.

257 Arendt, H. (1958) 'What was authority?', *NOMOS: Am. Soc'y Pol. Legal Phil.*, vol. 81, no. 1.

258 https://www.the-american-interest.com/2017/07/01/losing-nation-state

259 For an elaboration of this point, see Furedi (2021).

sciously questioned the desirability of transmitting their nation's historical legacy. In the United States, there has been a veritable crusade designed to de-authorise the status of the Founding Fathers and the very act of founding the nation. In British schools too, there is a discernible tendency to avoid public expressions of national pride. For example, a report authored by Michael Hand and Jo Pearce of the London-based Institute of Education argued that 'patriotism should not be taught in school.' Based on a survey of 300 teachers, the report concluded that patriotism should only be taught as a 'controversial issue'. Hand and Pearce went on to claim that Britain, with its 'morally ambiguous' history, should no longer be made into an object of school pupils' affection'[260]. Their study is not simply a critique of British national identity but also of loyalty to the tradition it embraces. They rhetorically asked, 'are countries really appropriate objects of love?' and called for implicit cultural hostility towards 'national histories', which are apparently 'morally ambiguous'. Their advice is that 'loving things can be bad for us', especially when the 'things we love are morally corrupt'. The message they communicated is that we should morally condemn any attempt to construct a British 'way of life'.

Three-quarters of the teachers surveyed by Hand and Pearce apparently agreed with the outlook of a patriotic-free education and said they felt they had an obligation to alert their pupils to the hazards of patriotic feelings. Although the authors subsequently complained about the 'press hysteria' evoked by their research, it is evident that they believed that their sentiment resonated with the times. They boasted that 'there are signs that the wave of patriotic rhetoric has now begun to break on the shores of public indifference'. After listing several failed official initiatives designed to boost British national identity, the reader was left in no doubt that the authors were convinced that they occupied the moral high ground[261].

It is evident that many schoolchildren have internalised Hand and Pearce's outlook. In April 2021, pupils at Pimlico Academy in South London protested against their school's policy of flying the Union Jack. Following the pattern of defeatism of recent decades, the school swiftly caved in to the children's demand to take down the 'racist' Union flag[262]. What is truly remarkable is not merely the moral cowardice of the school leaders, who refused to uphold and defend this

---

260 Cited in 'Patriotism "should not be taught in schools"', *The Daily Telegraph*, 1 February 2008.

261 Hand, M., and Pearce, J. (2009) 'Patriotism in British schools: Principles, practices and press hysteria', *Educational Philosophy and Theory*, vol. 41, no. 4, p. 465.

262 https://www.telegraph.co.uk/news/2021/04/01/principal-caves-protesting-students-removes-racist-union-jack

symbol of Britishness but also that the headteacher apologised and actually praised the students' behaviour! 'Our students are bright, courageous, intelligent young people, passionate about the things that matter to them and acutely attuned to injustice. I admire them hugely for this though I regret that it came to this', wrote Daniel Smith, the headteacher[263].

Smith and some of the other school leaders were likely aware of the serious implications of a state of affairs where a school in England is forced to take down the Union Jack. But instead of addressing this issue, Smith deflected the problem by stating, 'we acknowledge that this symbol is a powerful one which evokes often intense reactions'. That's another way of saying that an expression of hatred for Britain is an understandable 'intense reaction'. In effect, the school's response to this incident indicated that it is prepared to live in a world where expressions of hatred for the symbol of the nation exist on the same moral plane as that of British identity.

Sections of the Anglo-American cultural elites welcome the decomposition of national identity. 'Britain is undergoing a full-blown identity crisis', gloated a *New York Times* reporter before adding, that it is a "hollowed-out country," "ill at ease with itself," "deeply provincial," and engaged in a "controlled suicide"[264]. Media commentators working for the BBC – the nation's public broadcasting outlet often snigger at displays of patriotism. They associate the flying of the flag with outdated provincialism.[265].

Over the decades, the disparagement of patriotism in schools means that children and a section of adult society have become steadily unmoored from their cultural roots. This sentiment has influenced the elites to the point that they have a weak sense of national purpose and identity. A sense of defeatism towards upholding a way of life was already evident since the 1960s, when the ruling classes of many Western societies failed to meet the challenge posed by the counterculture. At the time, neither the American nor the British political class could provide a persuasive account of a way of life that could help society forge a sense of unity. In the case of Britain, the erosion of its national identity became strikingly evident in the post-Cold War era.

Confusion and loss of confidence about moral purpose do not only have implications for the constitution of moral clarity. The absence of an overarching moral purpose in society directly undermines a nation's sense of security. This

263 Read more: https://metro.co.uk/2021/04/01/pimlico-academy-headteacher-vows-to-change-racist-uniform-rules-14339725/?ito=cbshare

264 https://www.nytimes.com/2017/11/04/sunday-review/britain-identity-crisis.html

265 https://www.telegraph.co.uk/politics/2021/03/20/bbc-labour-share-nasty-problem-patriotism/

problem became evident during the so-called War on Terror in the post-9/11 era. According to Gwyn Prins and Robert Salisbury, the UK 'presents itself as a target, as a fragmenting, post-Christian society, increasingly divided about interpretations of its history, about its national aims, its values and its political identity'. They contend that 'the country's lack of self-confidence is in stark contrast to the implacability of its Islamist enemy, within and without'[266]. This acknowledgement of cultural insecurities in the face of the War on Terror serves as testimony to the absence of clarity about what values, if any, bind people together. Although such concerns have as their focus on national security in this instance, cultural conflicts also directly express themselves through anxieties about individual identity and the troubles of everyday life.

The unravelling of the normative foundation for public life has created a condition where values become a source of conflict instead of serving as an instrument for achieving unity. This fragmentation has diminished the capacity of the ruling elites to acquire the capacity to act as a cohesive and purposeful group. Conflicts over values leading to a palpable sense of disunity have important security and geopolitical consequences. This problem becomes particularly serious when the lines between domestic cultural politics and the pursuit of foreign affairs become blurred. Divisions over culture threaten to subordinate the interests of the people of Ukraine to one side or other in the Western culture war.

In the post-Cold War years, a morally disarmed European elite evaded facing the challenge of dealing with the many issues surrounding national security. That is why the nations of Western Europe find themselves in a situation where they lack the capacity necessary to defend themselves when confronted with the spectre of war on their continent. The belated attempt by EU leaders to adopt the policy of 'strategic autonomy' exposes the absence of precisely the kind of capacities necessary for the defence of its security[267]. Having outsourced responsibility for its military defence to the United States, Europe is forced to rearm itself. Even Germany, which has been most hesitant on this score, has opted to increase its spending on defence. However, spending on defence is not enough; the West also needs to rearm morally.

---

266 Prins & Salisbury (2008), p. 4.
267 https://www.robert-schuman.eu/en/european-issues/0620-european-sovereignty-strategic-au
tonomy-europe-as-a-power-what-reality-for-the-european-union

Chapter 6
Ukraine and the Myth of the Great Reset

It is difficult to write a concluding chapter to this book in May 2022, when the war it is describing seems far from over. Some may think it better to wait until we are in a better position to reflect with the wisdom of hindsight that is not yet available. But tomorrow is too late to begin to draw some of the obvious conclusions that are evident now. Lack of all the evidence is no excuse. The consequences of historical amnesia, the folly of Endism and the neglect of the importance of traditional boundaries, both national and cultural, have led to the moral disarmament of the West. These are issues that we need to start discussing now.

The unexpected military setbacks suffered by Russia in Ukraine have been seized upon by governments and commentators as an opportunity for revitalising the West. That is why the war in Ukraine was widely acclaimed as the beginning of a new era; as the 'crucible of the new world order'[268]. Some see it as a new beginning. The German Chancellor Olaf Scholz stated that with Russia's invasion of Ukraine the world stands in a 'new era'. He announced an 'historic shift' in German defence policy and indicated that 100 billion euros was to be invested in the army in 2022 alone[269].

From the perspective of the outlook of Endism, the war in Ukraine heralds the 'Great Reset'. According to one source 'Ukraine accelerates the Great Reset'[270]! The Great Reset is a fantasy scenario invented by Klaus Schwab, the founder of the World Economic Forum. Back in June 2020 he argued that the COVID pandemic provided a compelling reason for the pursuit of a 'great reset of capitalism'. For Schwab, the Great Reset represented the realisation of the globalist vision of a reorganised global capitalism. Many argue that the invasion of Ukraine provides an unanswerable argument for the Great Reset[271].

Whatever the Great Reset may mean, it is a metaphor that signifies the coming of a new era and the end of the old. This sentiment is communicated in a variety of different ways. 'The invasion of Ukraine is a paradigm shift on the scale of 9/11', British Foreign Minister Liz Truss told an audience in Washington

---

268 https://www.theguardian.com/world/2022/mar/12/how-ukraine-has-become-the-crucible-of-the-new-world-order

269 https://www.france24.com/en/live-news/20220227-a-new-era-germany-rewrites-its-defence-foreign-policies

270 https://asiatimes.com/2022/03/ukraine-accelerates-the-great-reset/

271 https://www.deseret.com/2022/3/11/22971239/how-russias-invasion-of-ukraine-has-changed-the-conversation-about-the-great-reset-crypto-glenn-beck

https://doi.org/10.1515/9783110981544-008

on March 10. She added, 'how we respond today will set the pattern for this new era'[272]. For Truss, the paradigm shift referred to 'fundamentally changing the way free democracies approach global security'[273]. Others use the term, 'A New World Order' to capture the phenomenon of a great reset. For President Biden, a New World Order means re-establishing American global hegemony. A New World Order is an aspiration rather than a reality for others. Ukrainian presidential advisor Andrity Yermak has warned:

'The current international security system has nearly expired. It's rotted through. Its remains have collapsed and buried the world order beneath. Trying to revive it is futile.
Most of all it resembles a broken automaton: its limbs are still able to move, but its gears are worn out, its springs are stretched. And the synchronicity that used to give perfection to its movements, has long gone.'[274]

Yermak's warning about the exhaustion of the prevailing international security system was coupled with the demand for a new arrangement. But the exhaustion of globalisation and the world order associated with it does not necessarily mean that a new one has emerged to take its place.

But as tempting as it is to perceive Ukraine as the crucible of the new world order, we are still at a very early stage of what many refer to as a 'new era'. We may be in a moment of transition, but there is little clarity about what we are transitioning towards. The global balance of power is unsettled, and many of the major players are far from clear about their direction of travel. Superficially, we have been here before and as the astute Washington-based commentator N.S. Lyons points out, it is much more accurate to interpret 'the beginning of a new era' as a 'rebirth in a new form of the old one that spent much of the last two decades crumbling apart'[275].

It certainly appears that the US government is enthusiastic about recreating the old American-dominated world order in a new form. It has adopted a policy of leading the charge against Russia. At least on the level of rhetoric, America's war aim is to defeat and humiliate Russia. At times Washington appears to use the war in Ukraine to achieve its own objectives. The former senior advisor to the Secretary of Defense in the Trump Administration, Col. Doug Macgregor, outlined his assessment of Washington's position in the following terms:

272 https://www.foreignaffairs.com/articles/ukraine/2022-05-04/war-ukraine-calls-reset-bidens-foreign-policy
273 https://www.theguardian.com/politics/2022/mar/09/ukraine-war-marks-paradigm-shift-on-the-scale-of-911-says-liz-truss
274 https://time.com/6171833/ukraine-global-system-failed
275 https://theupheaval.substack.com/p/the-world-order-reset?s=r_

'Well at this point we have to conclude that there is a universal opposition to any peace arrangement that involves a recognition of any Russian success. ... In fact if anything, it looks more and more, as though Ukrainians are almost incidental to the operation in the sense that they are there to impale themselves on the Russian army. And die in great numbers, because the real goal of this entire thing is the destruction of the Russian state and Vladimir Putin.'[276]

Macgregor's cynical assessment of America's war aim is shared by other Washington-based experts. Leon Panetta, former director of the CIA (2009–11) and Secretary of Defense under the Barack Obama regime, explained in March 2022:

'The only way to basically deal with Putin right now is to double down ourselves. Which means to provide as much military aid as necessary to the Ukrainians so that they can continue the battle against the Russians. ... We are engaged in a conflict here. It is a proxy war with Russia whether we say so or not. That effectively is what is going on. And for that reason, we have to be sure we are providing as much weaponry as possible. ... Make no mistake about it, diplomacy is going nowhere unless we have leverage. And the way you get leverage is by frankly going in and killing Russians. That is what the Ukrainians have to do. We have to continue the war effort. ... Because this is a power game.'[277]

Not only did Panetta forgot to mention that 'going in and killing Russians' would likely necessitate the loss of thousands and thousands of Ukrainian lives – he also failed to acknowledge that the waging of a proxy war by the United States against Russia signals that Washington's war aims do not necessarily align with Ukraine's. In effect, what we have are two wars running in parallel: Russia's war against Ukraine, where Ukraine is fighting a defensive battle for securing the nation's sovereignty; and America and some of her allies' proxy war against Russia, the aim of which is to reduce Russia's global power substantially.

It is important to note that the aim of defending the border and sovereignty of Ukraine is not synonymous with defeating and humiliating Russia. Supporting Ukraine to defend itself is essential for upholding its sovereignty and independence. However, no one's interest – including that of Ukraine – is served by imposing a crushing and humiliating defeat on Russia. This point was well observed by Henry Kissinger when he told those in attendance at the May 2022 meeting of Davos that such a crushing defeat would have disastrous consequen-

---

276 https://www.realclearpolitics.com/video/2022/03/16/macgregor_washington_wants_war_ to_continue_as_long_as_possible_in_hopes_to_overthrown_putin.htm
277 https://www.bloomberg.com/news/videos/2022-03-17/u-s-is-in-a-proxy-war-with-russia-pan etta-video

ces for the long-term stability of Europe[278]. What concerned Kissinger was that if the West did not recognise Russia's role in the European balance of power, an era of permanent conflict would ensue. Kissinger's warning was echoed by Yehezekel Dror, one of Israel's leading foreign-policy scholars, who stated that calling Putin a war criminal was a form of 'strategic madness'[279].

Questions about America's war aims were also raised in a *New York Times* editorial:

'Is the United States, for example, trying to help bring an end to this conflict, through a settlement that would allow for a sovereign Ukraine and some kind of relationship between the United States and Russia? Or is the United States now trying to weaken Russia permanently? Has the administration's goal shifted to destabilizing Vladimir Putin or having him removed? Does the United States intend to hold Mr. Putin accountable as a war criminal? Or is the goal to try to avoid a wider war—and if so, how does crowing about providing U.S. intelligence to kill Russians and sink one of their ships achieve this?'[280]

In effect, America's proxy war against Russia subordinates Ukraine's cause to a global power-play. America's attempt to re-establish global hegemony at the expense of Russia is also unrealistic. It is a policy that leaves China and much of the non-Western world out of the equation. It is a short-sighted strategy that is likely to set in motion a chain of events leading to further global conflict.

Outwardly, the war in Ukraine has provided a focus for the consolidation of Western unity and the rebirth of NATO as a credible force. However, the longer the war continues, the more it becomes evident that members of the Western alliance have conflicting war aims. While Washington claimed that it was interested in nothing less than the defeat of Russia, at different times, the leaders of France, Italy and Germany talked of seeking a ceasefire, even if it meant Ukraine ceding some of her territory[281]. Despite all the talk about the revival of the West, genuine unity cannot be forged based on forcing Russia onto the defensive. As we noted previously, the project of recreating the glory days of the Cold War cannot succeed in the current multipolar world.

The aspiration for a New World Order needs to reckon with the reality that a one-sided focus on Russia distracts from other points of conflict. We have seen a

278 https://www.telegraph.co.uk/business/2022/05/23/henry-kissinger-warns-against-defeat-russia-western-unity-sanctions
279 https://www.bloomberg.com/opinion/articles/2022-05-14/ukraine-s-allies-are-blundering-their-handling-of-russia-s-putin
280 https://www.nytimes.com/2022/05/19/opinion/america-ukraine-war-support.html
281 https://www.telegraph.co.uk/world-news/2022/05/22/western-resolve-set-tested-key-us-eu-figures-want-ukraine-cede

major shift in how geopolitics works since the end of the Cold War. The world has gone from a bipolar to a unipolar and finally to a nonpolar global reality. This trend has rendered geopolitics and international affairs more fluid and less predictable. During the pandemic, these trends have intensified and have significantly undermined the effectiveness of many international institutions that emerged in the post-World War Two era.

In recent decades, the most significant geopolitical development has been the decline of American global hegemony. Washington's anxiety about the decline of American economic power was intensified in the wake of the 2008/9 financial crisis. America and other Western nations had to rely on China to help them contain the destructive consequences of this crisis. The shifting balance of power in the world economy led America to attempt to hold back China's economic and technological ascendancy by emphasising military containment. Aukus, the new security alliance between the US, Britain and Australia, expressed the refocusing of geopolitical strategy toward the Asia-Pacific region.

The war in Ukraine is paralleled not simply by a proxy war but also by a domestic-oriented culture war. In the United States and other parts of the Western world, the conflict in Ukraine is often interpreted through the prism of its Culture War. The war was preceded in January 2022 by President Biden's Summit for Democracy. One of the aims of this conference was to repose global tensions as a battle between Biden-type democracy and the forces of populism and authoritarianism. The moralistic dichotomy that the Biden administration draws between the forces of Good and Evil is, as one observer noted, 'unconvincing in light of Washington's support for many autocratic governments'[282]. The claim of the Biden administration to be on the side of the angels in democracy-autocracy divide is continually called into question by its willingness to forge close alliances with governments, such as that of Saudi Arabia. Washington is very selective in its use of the label authoritarian. Despite its constant moralising, Washington is forced to engage in a measure of *realpolitik*. As one commentator in *The Financial Times* observed, 'The US will need the help of some illiberal states to prevail over Russia and China'[283].

In the current unsettled global environment, the declaration that a New World Order has arrived is premature. Informed by the outlook of endism that we discussed previously, it is motivated by the impulse of escaping from the past. This is not quite as smooth as it could be. Paying greater heed to the unresolved issues of the past is far more rewarding than looking for solutions from an

---

282 https://www.foreignaffairs.com/articles/world/2022-01-10/democracy-talk-cheap
283 https://www.ft.com/content/182adfa1-daae-449a-bdd9-8fe4265c20ed

invented new era. Those who perceive Ukraine through the metaphor of a Great Reset need to understand that you cannot reboot human society. It is possible to reset 'something mechanical or physical' but not history![284]

The War — No End in Sight

The war in Ukraine presents itself as different to other wars. For a start, there has not even been a declaration of war. Putin refers to it as a 'special operation', while Western governments supporting Ukraine have been extremely careful not to cross a line that would lead to war. It looks as if this is a war that neither side can win nor dare lose. The issues in play are existential since what is at stake is Ukraine's status as a sovereign nation and the integrity and survival of the Russian Federation. At the time of writing – end of May 2022 – it looks like neither side is capable of inflicting a decisive victory over the other. Russia may consolidate its pre-war position in Eastern Ukraine, and Ukraine can thwart Putin's ambition and survive as an independent nation. That would represent a moral victory for Ukraine. However, it will not result in a durable peace, whatever the short-term outcome. Both sides know that a ceasefire will be temporary and serve as a prelude to an outbreak of conflict in what has since 2014 been a classical frontier war.

Matters are complicated by the current state of global instability, one where the world order is undermined by the absence of clarity about the balance of power.

Geopolitical illiteracy and the state of historical amnesia prevailing in the West lead to a short-sighted preoccupation with domestic concerns. Bogged down in a state of presentism, its rhetoric of a new normal, a New World Order, or a Great Reset is devoid of any serious content. There is something truly infantile about the constant refrain of endism. Stumbling in the dark, the West is in danger of being trapped in its presentist swamp.

In 1938, Winston Churchill published a book titled *Arms and Covenant*, which was later that year republished in the U.S. under the title *While England Slept: A Survey of World Affairs, 1932–1938*[285]. Churchill was furious at the reluctance of the British government to take seriously the threat posed by Nazi Ger-

---

284 See OED Online. March 2022. Oxford University Press. https://www-oed-com.chain.kent.ac. uk/view/Entry/163522?rskey=weR36b&result=2

285 See Churchill, W.S. (2016) *While England Slept: A Survey Of World Affairs, 1932–1938*, Ishi Press: New York.

many and its failure to prepare the military for the war to come. Hitler's invasion of Poland vindicated his call to rearm.

Were Churchill alive today, his version of *While England Slept* would be re-titled *While the West Went into Hibernation*. What mattered in 1938 was to rearm militarily to confront a grave threat to human civilisation. What matters today is not so much military but moral rearmament. On the road to Ukraine, the West took a wrong turn and lost its way. Having consciously become detached from its past, it became indifferent to the need to preserve the values that provided the foundation of its civilisation. In effect, the West morally disarmed itself to the point that it now needs to harness the heroism of the people of Ukraine for the self-serving project of revitalising itself. Ukrainians deserve much more than that. They are not fighting for their lives to make Western politicians feel good about themselves.

Western societies will have to learn that you cannot pause or delete history. As the war in Ukraine illustrates, the past caches up with us sooner or later.

Recovering its sense of historical consciousness is the precondition for the Western world to acquire the ability to play a mature and responsible role in global affairs.

Bibliography

Adams, H. (2019) *The Education of Henry Adams*, Good Press: New York.

Arendt, H. (1958) 'What was Authority?', *NOMOS: American Society*, vol. 81, no. 1.

Arendt, H. (1998) *The Human Condition*, The University of Chicago Press: Chicago.

Beck, U. (2002) 'The cosmopolitan society and its enemies', *Theory, culture & society*, vol. 19, nos. 1–2.

Beck, U. (2003) 'Understanding the real Europe', *Dissent*, vol. 50, no. 3.

Beck, U. (2005) *Power In the Global Age: A New Global Political Economy*, Polity Press: Cambridge.

Beck, U. (2006) *The Cosmopolitan Vision*. Polity Press: Cambridge.

Bennett, W.J. (2003) *Why We Fight. Moral Clarity and the War on Terrorism*, Regnery Publishing Inc: Washington, D.C.

Berger, S. (2007) 'Writing National Histories in Europe: Reflections on the Pasts, Presents and Futures of a Tradition' in Jarusch, K.H., and Lindenberger, T. (eds.) *Conflicted Memories: Europeanizing Contemporary Histories*, Berghahn Books: Oxford.

Bosniak, L. (1999) 'Citizenship denationalized', *Indiana Journal of Global Legal Studies*, vol. 7, no. 2.

Bracher, K.D. (1984) *The Age of Ideologies*, Weidenfeld and Nicholson: London.

Canovan, M. (1996) *Nationhood and Political Theory*, Edward Elgar: Cheltenham.

Canovan, M. (1999) 'Is there an Arendtian case for the nation-state?', *Contemporary Politics*, vol. 5, no. 2.

Churchill, W. (1930) *My Early Life*, London: Thornton Butterworth Limited.

Churchill, W.S. (2016) *While England Slept: A Survey Of World Affairs, 1932–1938*, Ishi Press: New York.

Coker, C. (2002) *Waging war without warriors? The changing culture of military conflict*, Lynne Rienner Publishers: Boulder, CO.

Coker, C. (2007) *The Warrior Ethos*, Routledge: London.

Coker, C. (2009) *War In An Age of Risk*, Polity Press: Cambridge.

Duffield, J.S. (1994) 'Explaining the Long Peace in Europe: the contributions of regional security regimes', *Review of International Studies*, vol. 20, no. 4.

Eilstrup-Sangiovanni, M., and Verdier, D. (2005) 'European integration as a solution to war', *European Journal of International Relations*, vol. 11.

Eksteins, M. (1989) *Rites of Spring: The Great War and the Birth of the Modern Age*, Houghton Mifflin: Boston.

Fukuyama (1992) *The End of History and the Last Man*, Free Press: New York.

Fukuyama, F. (2006) *The End of History and the Last Man*, Simon and Schuster: New York.

Furedi, F. (2007) *Invitation To Terror: The Expanding Empire Of The Unknown*, Bloomsbury: London.

Furedi, F. (2014) *First World War – Still No End In Sight*, Bloomsbury: London.

Furedi, F. (2018) *Populism And The European Culture Wars: The Conflict of Values between Hungary and the EU*, Routledge: London.

Furedi, F. (2021) *100 Years of Identity Crisis: The Culture War Over Socialisation*, De Gruyter: Berlin.

Fussell, P. (1975) *The Great War and Modern memory*, Oxford University Press: Oxford.

Gamble, A. (2013) *Politics and Fate*. Wiley: London.

https://doi.org/10.1515/9783110981544-009

Habermas, J. (1988) 'Historical consciousness and post-traditional identity: remarks on the Federal Republic's Orientation to the West', *Acta Sociologica*, vol. 31, no. 1.

Habermas, J. (2016) *The Crisis of the European Union*, Polity Press: Cambridge.

Hand, M., and Pearce, J. (2009) 'Patriotism in British schools: Principles, practices and press hysteria', *Educational Philosophy and Theory*, vol. 41, no. 4.

Hartog, F. (2017) *Regimes of Historicity: Presentism And Experiences of Time*, Columbia University Press: New York.

Howard, M. (1991) *The Lessons of History*, Clarendon Press: Oxford.

Inglehart, R.F., Puranen, B., and Welzel, C. (2015) 'Declining willingness to fight for one's country: The individual-level basis of the long peace', *Journal of Peace Research*, vol. 52, no. 4.

Inglis, D. (2010) 'The death of history in British sociology: Presentism, intellectual entrepreneurship and the conundra of historical consciousness' in Burnett, J., Jeffers, S., and Thomas, G. (eds.) *New Social Connections: Sociology's Subjects and Objects*, Palgrave: Basingstoke.

Judt, T. (2009) *Reappraisals: Reflections On A Forgotten Century*, Vintage Books: London.

Kahl, C., and Wright, T. (2021) *Aftershocks: Pandemic Politics and the End of the Old International Order*, St Martin's Press: New York.

Kaiser, W. (2015) 'Clash of Cultures: Two Milieus in the European Union—A New Narrative For Europe Project', *Journal of Contemporary European Studies*, vol. 12, no. 3.

Kaldor, M. (1999) *New and Old Wars: Organised Violence in a Global Era*, Polity Press: Cambridge.

Lachmann, R. (2020) *First-Class Passengers on a Sinking Ship: Elite Politics and the Decline of Great Powers*, Verso: London.

Lacquement Jr, R.A. (2004) 'The Casual-Aversion Myth', *Naval War College Review*, vol. 57.

Laidi, Z. (1998) *A World Without Meaning: The Crisis Of Meaning In International Politics*, Routledge: London.

Lasch, C. (1995), *Revolt of the Elites: And The Betrayal of Democracy*, W.W. Norton: New York.

Lasch, C. (2018) *The Culture of Narcissism: American life in an age of diminishing expectations*. WW Norton & Company: New York.

Leonard, M., Small, A. and Rose, M. (2005) *British Public Diplomacy in the "Age of Schisms"*, The Foreign Policy Centre: London.

Martín-Arroyo, P. (2015) *"Histoeuropeanisation": Challenges and Implications of (Re)writing the History of Europe "Europeanly", 1989–2015*, College of Europe Natolin Campus: Warszawa.

Mayer, A.J. (1969) 'Internal Causes and Purposes of War in Europe, 1870–1956: A Research Assignment', *The Journal of Modern History*, vol. 41, no. 3.

McNeill, W.H. (1989) 'Winds of change', *Foreign Affairs*, vol. 69.

Meier, C. (2005) *The Uses of History: From Athens to Auschwitz*, Harvard University Press: Cambridge, Mass.

Markides, C. (2021) *Organizing for the New Normal*, Kogan Page: London.

Meyerson, A. (1990) 'The Vision Thing Continued', *Policy Review*.

Mizruchi, M.S., and Hyman, M. (2014) 'Elite fragmentation and the decline of the United States', *Political Power and Social Theory*, vol. 26.

Möhring, J. & Prins, G. (2013) *Sail On, O Ship Of State*, Notting Hill Editions: London.

Moran, D. (2012) *Husserl's Crisis of the European Sciences and Transcendental Phenomenology: An Introduction*, Cambridge University Press: Cambridge.

Mueller, J. (2004) *The remnants of war*, Cornell University Press: Ithaca.

Mueller, J.E. (2006) *Overblown: How politicians and the terrorism industry inflate national security threats, and why we believe them*, Simon and Schuster: New York.

Müller, J-W. (2013) *Contesting Democracy: Political Ideas In Twentieth Century Europe*, Yale University Press: New Haven.

Neumann, P. & Smith, M.L.R, (2005) 'Missing the plot? Intelligence and discourse failure', *Orbis*, vol. 49, no. 1.

Nietzsche, F. (1967) *The Will To Power*, Random House: New York.

Nussbaum, M. (2002) 'Patriotism and Cosmopolitanism' in Nussbaum, M. (ed.) *For Love of Country*, Beacon Press: Boston.

O'Dowd, L. (2010) 'From a "Borderless World" to a "World of Borders"; bringing history back in', *Environment and Planning D: Society and Space*, vol. 28, no. 6.

Pfaff, W. (1990) *Barbarian Sentiments: How the American Century Ends*, The Noonday Press: New York.

Pharr, S.J., Putnam, R.D., and Dalton, R.J. (2000) 'A Quarter-Century of Declining Confidence', *Journal of Democracy*, vol. 11.

Plumb, J.H. (1969) *The Death of The Past*, Macmillan: London.

Prins, G., and Salisbury, R. (2008) *Risk, Threat and Security: The case of the United Kingdom*, RUSI: London.

Prozorov, S., (2008) 'De-limitation: the denigration of boundaries in the political thought of late modernity', in Parker, N. (ed.) *The Geopolitics of Europe's Identity: Centres, Boundaries and Margins*, Palgrave Macmillan: London.

Reinhart, C., and Reinhart, V. (2020) 'The pandemic depression: The global economy will never be the same', *Foreign Affairs*, vol. 99.

Rich, P. (1989) 'Imperial Decline and the resurgence of British national identity' in Kushner, T., and Lunn, K. (eds.) *Traditions of Intolerance*, Manchester University Press: Manchester.

Rosa, H. (2013) 'Conclusion: Frenetic Standstill? The End of History' in Rosa, H. (ed.) *Social Acceleration*, Columbia University Press: New York.

Siegel, M.L. (2004) *The moral disarmament of France: education, pacifism, and patriotism, 1914–1940* (No. 18), Cambridge University Press: Cambridge.

Slobodian, Q. (2018) *Globalists: The End of Empire And The Birth Of NeoLiberalism*, Harvard University Press: Cambridge, Mass.

Thomas, B. (1991) *The new historicism: and other old-fashioned topics*, Princeton University Press: Princeton, NJ.

Tooze, A. (2018) *Crashed: How a Decade of Financial Crises Changed the World*, Allen Lane: London.

Turner, B.S. (ed.) (1993) *Citizenship and Social Theory*, Sage: London.

von Hagen, M. (1995), 'Does Ukraine Have a History?', *Slavic Review*, vol. 54.

Weber, M. (1915) 'Religious rejections of the world and their directions' in Gerth, H.H., and Wright Mills, C.W. (eds.) (1958) *From Max Weber: Essays in Sociology*, Galaxy Books: New York.

Wolczuk, K. (2001) *The Moulding of Ukraine: the constitutional politics of state formation*, Central European University Press: Budapest.

Yuval-Davis, Y., Wemyss, G., and Cassidy, K. (2019) *Bordering*, Polity Press: Cambridge.

Zimmermann, K.F., Karabulut, G., Bilgin, M.H., and Doker, A.C. (2020) 'Inter-country distancing, globalisation and the coronavirus pandemic', *The World Economy*, vol. 43, no. 6.